Practical Carving

Practical Carving

in wood, stone, plastics and other materials

Robert Dawson

Studio Vista London

Acknowledgements

The author thanks all who have helped him by providing photographs, or facilities for taking photographs. These include staff and students of Kennington City and Guilds School of Art; Sir John Cass Fine Art Department; Central London Polytechnic; Raydon Modern School, Suffolk, especially Jean Barnes, in charge of the art department; J. Bysouth Ltd and William Knight and Co. Ltd, Masons and Stone Merchants; Eric Gowlland; Mike Srawley; and many more private individuals and firms who have assisted not only with photographs but also with invaluable information and advice.

Frontispiece—*Falling Figure* by
Robert Dawson

© Robert Dawson 1972
First published in Great Britain 1972 by
Studio Vista Publishers, Blue Star House, Highgate Hill, London N 19
and in the United States of America 1972 by
Watson-Guptill Publications, 165 West 46th Street, New York, NY 10036

Set in Garamond 11pt 1pt leaded
Photoset and printed in Great Britain by
BAS Printers Limited, Wallop, Hampshire

ISBN 0 289 70109 0

Contents

Foreword

Fig. 1 *Job* by H. Nonnenmacher (Berlin 1925). Oak, height 100 cm. (39 ins.)

Carving is the exact opposite of modelling. The sculptor modelling with clay or some other malleable material starts from the inside and works steadily outwards, until eventually he arrives at the outside surface. The carver does the reverse—he starts with a block of material, and cuts away until he arrives at the sculpture contained within the block.

The ability to look into a block and see contained in it a form, then to set about peeling off the surplus material surrounding it, demands an effort of three-dimensional imagination that is not often achieved without practice. Occasionally people have it inborn, or have developed it early for themselves, but for most of us it is an ability that we develop slowly. Modelling also demands a three-dimensional awareness of what the end product will be; but as we build, the awareness of what we are achieving grows as the sculpture develops, while the production of a carving, generally speaking, requires a much greater awareness of what the final result will be.

Here lies the challenge—we live in a three-dimensional world, but often we conceive in two dimensions only. How much can we train ourselves to feel in three dimensions? Developing a three-dimensional awareness is not all that carving does; it helps us to appreciate the quality of materials—their texture, colour, density, what they will do, how they are manipulated, what they are capable of.

This book starts with a discussion of carving in general—methods, types, and problems of designing—and then goes on to describe the main media, the methods of working them, and some briefer notes on the less popular materials. Many of these materials can be carved by children, some by the very young. Most are capable of being treated with great sophistication. This range of complexity means that carving is within the capacity of anyone who wants to carve. The same applies to tools and equipment; carving can be done with the very simplest tools or the most sophisticated.

Today carving is much less popular than it used to be. The process is often too long for present-day requirements. It is true that the result of carving is not instant art, but by dropping it from the repertoire a part of experience is lost.

7

Introduction

Materials

Carving is an art that can be practised from a very young age, almost as early as painting. Many materials are capable of being used by young children, adult beginners and professionals, all with their own degree of sophistication. Some are more limited in their range and can only be used with a high degree of technical skill. But the range is so great that there are plenty of media to suit everyone.

The simplest materials are blocks of salt and blocks of soap. It is not easy to find block salt nowadays, but if it can be obtained, it is ideal for a young child. It can be carved with a spoon, a stick or anything else available.

Soap is slightly less easy to use, but even so it is easily scraped with a spoon. It can also be carved with great intricacy and detail, so it covers a wide range of ability.

Plaster of paris and chalk are two materials that are easy to work. They are inclined to be messy, but small blocks worked on a table will not cause too much trouble.

Wood is probably the favourite carving material for the amateur. It is clean, beautiful, usually smells good, and is satisfying to work. There is an enormous variety of types, each with its own characteristics and quality. Simple carvings can be made without using chisels and gouges at all. Much can be achieved with rasp, saw and file. A few gouges make the process more exciting. These tools, as sharp as razors, are a delight to use, and safe when used properly.

Choose your first blocks of wood with some care. Many of the woods work well; but some woods, such as beech, are so hard and dense that not only are they a great trial of patience for the beginner, but tools may well be damaged. A firm but more easily worked wood is a better choice: lime, the wood traditionally used by German woodcarvers; mahogany, harder but clean and readily worked; pine, for very simple shapes.

Quite young children can work the softer limestones. Some of them are so soft that they can be scraped with metal tools, but it is better to give them mallet-headed claw tools and chisels, or old wood-working gouges, because this is the traditional way to work stone, and it is satisfying for a child to learn to handle mallet and chisel. Apart from these simple materials, carving a sculpture in stone requires some degree of patience and consistent application. The hardest stones can only be chipped away in small flakes, and even with the aid of mechanical tools the process is slow and patient. A large granite sculpture may take a man a year or more of hard, consistent work by hand. Set against this is the sense of achievement at having mastered a hard, intractable material.

Most people will be satisfied with easier materials, or smaller sculptures made from the very hard materials. It is wise to start with an easy material, say a soft or medium limestone, and, when practised in the handling of tools, to progress to the harder materials, which are capable of taking finer finishes.

Of the other materials, concrete building block and brick can be used by both children and adults. Red bricks can be filed and scraped and glasspapered, or even worked with sharp chisel. This applies also to building block.

On the other hand these materials can be treated with considerable sophistication, and on a large scale. Henry Moore's brick reliefs in Rotterdam, Holland, are examples.

Sculptures in acrylic and ivory are not usually large. Neither material is difficult to work.

It is neither possible nor useful to list and classify everything carveable. Some materials are obviously unsuitable for the beginner. The most important task is to discover what the particular material is capable of. Trial and experiment are the chief means of doing so, allied to adequate instruction. All materials vary in their potential. Some vary from block to block. 'Respect for the material' is an over-used cliché. Sometimes, by careful work, it is possible to stretch the capacity of the material beyond what could be expected. Nevertheless, the discovery of what a material will reasonably do, what is excessively difficult and time-wasting, and what makes a material unsuitable for a particular job, is an important part of education—not only that of the sculptor, but of all of us.

It is particularly important that this knowledge should be imparted to beginners, especially to children, both to educate them in an awareness of the proper use of materials, and to avoid disappointments, which may discourage them from persisting with carving.

Woodcarving, stonecarving, carving ivory, acrylic or anything else requires one kind of thinking. Most professionals do not limit themselves to one medium, and I would urge students to try more than one. It is a stimulating exercise, and the comparisons and differences between two materials increase the understanding of both.

Designing

The block

The carver starts with a block. Whether it is chosen to interpret a preconceived idea, or whether the block itself is the source of inspiration, at some point in time he will stand, chisel in hand, preparing to make the first cut.

The subject of design covers a vast area. Books are written about it, students spend years studying it. All we can do here is to raise a few general points and investigate those that refer specifically to carving.

Fig. 2 shows an ovoid form carved in hemlock (this and figs 7–10

Fig. 2 Ovoid form, student exercise. Hemlock

Fig. 3 Head (unfinished). Portland stone

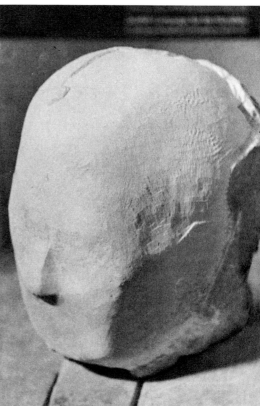

are examples from an exercise investigating the block, carried out by architecture students). The carving consisted of removing the corners and edges, working away the planes until only one point remained on each side that had, originally, touched the outside of the block. This example is the last of several carried out by the student.

The paradoxical truth is that the ovoid is a form arrived at via the simplification of more complex forms, and is not a starting point. Nevertheless it is reasonable to consider this simple, essentially convex form first of all, because it is closest to the block.

The difficulty of creating a meaningful sculpture in terms of the ovoid is the very simplicity of the form, which, unless subtle, sophisticated and tense, may only call for the comment 'So what?'.

The head is essentially ovoid and is full of meaning. With the head the form becomes less simple; the ovoid is more complex and less smooth. Concavities appear which become eye-sockets and hollows on either side of the nose. Fig 3 is an unfinished head carved in Portland stone. It is still almost completely convex—with just a few hollows.

This type of form owes little to the space around it. Any form must displace air, must create a space that is the negative of itself, but we are not very conscious of this space.

Fig. 4 Drawing of head. Student exercise, showing the essentially enclosed nature of these forms

Fig. 5 *Sleeping Muse* by Constantin Brancusi. Marble. Musée d'art Moderne, Paris. Photo courtesy Courtauld Institute of Art

Fig. 6 Skull, believed to be Aztec (Mexico). Rock crystal, fifteenth century. British Museum, London

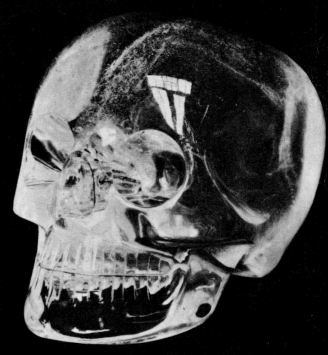

Figs 7–10 Carvings in hemlock and walnut (fig. 10). A student exercise to remove a given percentage of a block. Note in fig. 7 the retention of the sawn surface on one side as a textural feature; and that in fig. 9 the knot, which might have interfered with the form, is used as emphasis for a keypoint

Form, space

Fig. 7

Once hollows begin to be an important factor, the space outside the sculpture takes on a major significance. The play of convex and hollow, of light and shadow, over the surface of the sculpture stimulates and excites, while the flow of space around the figure becomes a part of the sculpture. Figs 7–10, examples of student exercises, were intended to manipulate form and space by the removal of a given percentage of material from a rectangular block. Look at the Cycladic sculpture (fig. 12), and notice how the shape of the carving is expressed by the way light falls upon it, but also how the profile becomes part of a lively, exciting shape. Cover half the figure vertically with a sheet of paper, and you will see that the space is as significant as the stone. The sculpture by Jean Arp in fig. 99 expresses this too, and is more clearly three-dimensional than the Cycladic figure. Remember that a two-dimensional photograph gives only a faint idea of the intricate flow of solid and void, and that every slight movement of the observer will bring fresh relationships into play. But every new view should satisfy. When I was a student my instructor remarked that if the silhouette of a sculpture is good, then the sculpture itself is probably good. This I believe to be true. The only thing that can spoil it is the superficial treatment of detail—or the inadequacy of the sculpture to fulfil the purpose for which it was created. This latter point will be discussed later.

Henry Moore once commented on the feeling of liberation when, as a student at the Royal College of Art, he first pushed a hole right through a sculpture. Space now flows not only round but through the carving; and the sculptor in imagination (and in fact, with his chisels), follows the space through the solid material. We are so used to spatial sculptures today that Henry Moore's statement seems strange to us. In African carving, fig. 72, the spaces are almost as significant as the forms. As material is removed, spaces become greater and the purpose of the form becomes more and more to manipulate the spaces, to define and control them.

Planes, curves, straights, junctions

Fig. 10 is composed exclusively of rectilinear elements. Any apparent line is, in fact, a change of direction of form through 90°.

In carving, a line invariably describes a change of direction, either as the junction of planes or as the limit of what can be seen on a curve, which means that at this point the plane ceases to be visible. (A plane is an area, either flat or curved, containing no major change of direction.)

Fig. 8

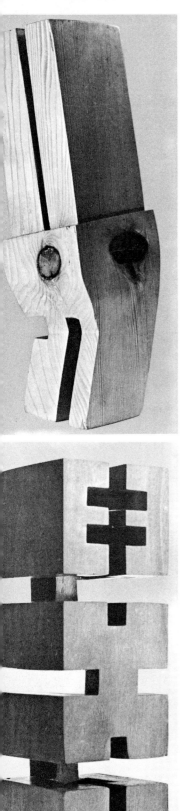

Fig. 9

The interplay of curves and straights, of concaves and convexes and hollow and high-point, is the sculptor's means of obtaining visual drama. African sculptors are masterly in their handling of these elements, and it was the study of African carving that inspired Picasso, Braque, Lipchitz and other major artists of the School of Paris at the beginning of the century.

One of the most important considerations in sculpture is how planes meet. In the example mentioned (fig. 10), all the junctions are simple, consisting of planes meeting at right-angles to each other. This is not often the case, however, and the sculptor is constantly having to make decisions as to how two (or more) planes will meet. It can be glossed over in impressionistic work, but where the work is firm and crisp, precise decisions have to be made. In any case, the junction should be capable of developing to precision. Examine junctions in the various illustrations throughout the book, and on actual carvings if possible, to understand how other carvers have solved these problems.

Light, shadow

It is by the manipulation of light that the carver expresses form; or perhaps I should say that we perceive form visually by the way light falls upon it. The depth and steepness of a hollow will control the amount of shadow it makes, given a constant light source. But light is not constant—natural light changes from hour to hour, and even minute to minute—and how a sculpture is placed affects how it will be lit, even under controlled conditions. This should be born in mind both when designing and during the carving process. Change the light to get as many varied light conditions as possible on the sculpture.

The sculptor manipulates his form to control light and shadow. By making a proper balance of form he expresses stability, strength, delicacy, fragility. One of the arts of designing is to give an appearance of delicacy to a relatively substantial and solid sculpture. This is done in two ways: firstly by so arranging the play of light and shadow that elements appear delicate when, in fact, they are quite substantial; and secondly, by so arranging fairly fine edges that they slope away and become much thicker, giving adequate support to themselves, but with the illusion of fragility.

There is a strong element of illusion in sculpture—in other words the artist makes the observer see what he wants him to see. For example, forms which are quite clearly differentiated in life become one in terms of sculpture and the junction will be treated non-naturalistically (fig. 27).

Fig. 10

Direction

The sculptor uses direction to control the way the observer looks at the sculpture, and also to express certain basic ideas: movement, violence, tension, tenderness, peace, etc. The spiral, used by Michaelangelo and taken up as the great theme of the Baroque artists, is the means they used to achieve the typical baroque drama. Drama is also achieved, but by different means in the Metope from the Parthenon (fig. 26). Note the sharp angularity of directions, which all speak of force and violence. The gesture of Job (fig. 1) bespeaks tension. The downward thrust of the arms against the upward curve of the legs, the horizontal of the shoulders stopping the V of the arms, the repetition of the stopped V in the neck and jaw, and the upward point of the face, all tell a story, not a literary story but one of emotions—resistance, suffering, tension.

The student should analyse sculptures in this way, whether historical or contemporary, figurative or abstract, to see how the sculptor has controlled his elements to express his concept. Remember that photographs tell only part of the story. One view is not enough—unless you are looking at a relief. Normally directions operate in three dimensions, not two.

A summary of other design factors

There are numerous other factors which have to be born in mind. While interdependent, they often have to be considered individually.

Fig. 11 Pencil study for the exercise in figs 7–10

SCALE

The governing factors are purpose, nature of material, cost, time available, function and proposed environment. To treat this aspect of design in a summary is an unfortunate necessity. A book could be written about scale alone. Many materials have a scale that is intrinsic (e.g. the size of a tusk or tooth); some are unsuitable for large sculptures, some for small. The former can sometimes be avoided by building with a number of units.

Where the sculpture is to be sited, and its purpose, will have an important bearing on scale. A sculpture intended for a small, enclosed space must differ in scale from one intended for a spacious open-air situation. A hand sculpture is different from a monument. Having stated the obvious, it should be realized that *every* sculpture has its appropriate size and this needs consideration.

COLOUR, TEXTURE

Materials are form; equally, materials are colour. To some extent colour and texture overlap. Smooth, polished surfaces are invariably

Fig. 12 Man playing a double flute, Cycladic, Crete. Stone, 2400–2200 BC. National Museum, Athens

darker than when left rough. By leaving areas of a sculpture rough and smoothing others, the same effect is achieved as painting would.

Painting sculpture is common, and used to be almost invariable. While adding emphasis, it has the effect of decreasing our awareness of the form. Maximum visual appreciation of form is obtained when the material is of one colour and directionally, but not violently, illuminated. One only has to think of the way a woman's make-up affects the face to realize what a controlling factor colour is.

CHOICE OF MATERIAL
Depends on availability, cost, facilities and necessary skills, where the sculpture will go, what its function is, and the scale. Qualities of the various materials are discussed in the appropriate sections.

15

Carving the block

Carving, by definition, consists of cutting away from a pre-existing block. The block may be natural or it may be made-up, but the process is one of taking away, as opposed to modelling, which is an additive process.

At one end of the scale carving drifts over into engraving, which consists of making scratches on the surface of a material. Work cannot be considered carving unless it consists of removing actual volumes of the material and changing, to some extent, the shape of the block. It may be that a particular block will inspire a form, and that the final form is similar to the shape of the original block. Nevertheless, material will be removed to refine and develop the form: this is carving.

Whether the sculptor has a clear idea of what he is going to carve, or whether his idea is tenuous and will evolve along with the carving, by the time he starts to carve he must be clear that certain volumes are to be removed. On an ivory carving these volumes may be tiny; on a stone sculpture they may be very big.

The first task is to remove them. The art of carving is to remove only what one is confident must be removed; but, knowing that this volume is waste, to cut it away with the minimum fuss and maximum speed. This means that a good deal of time is spent on contemplation and initial working out. Beginners are usually too eager to get down to the physical business of carving, but time spent in thinking out the initial moves is time well spent. It will not only save much time in the end, but will enable the sculptor to retain a much clearer idea of his intentions as the shape of the block changes and the sculpture develops.

How the initial blocking-out is done depends on the size, material and form of the sculpture. With large stone sculptures this may be done in part by machine in a mason's yard, or the sculptor himself may do it all, either with the help of mechanical tools, or with hand tools. Small sculptures will certainly be blocked-out by the sculptor himself.

Even if the sculpture is pierced and rather open in form, it is usual to develop the outside shape to some extent first of all.

A seated figure carved from a rectangular block

1 Draw a side view on the block. Cut away all surplus material right through.
2 Draw a front view, lining up important points carefully—chin, elbow, knees, etc. Cut away surplus from this view.

You will now be left with the block very cubey, but with the main masses cut away.

There will still be a large quantity of material to be cut away. Maybe two-thirds, maybe more of the volume will be removed before the figure is finished.

3 Examine the block carefully. Look at it from all angles, especially from above, and determine how the figure is contained within the block, particularly how and where parts of the final figure touch or nearly touch the outside of the block. Note, for example, where the crown of the head, the nose, the elbows, the knees, the toes, the shoulder blades, the buttocks, are positioned, and mark carefully on the block. If, in the course of carving, any of these marks are carved away because the points are below the surface, remark them in the appropriate place immediately.

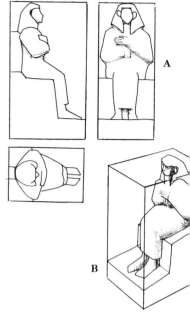

Fig. 15 Drawings showing how a figure fits into a rectangular block (based on Egyptian carving of the Steward Hetep, Twelfth Dynasty, 1950 BC)
A side elevation, front elevation and plan (note how small the legs appear in the front view, due to lack of perspective)
B perspective drawing

Fig. 16
A boasting drawing
B blocking-out

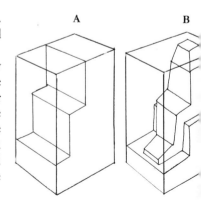

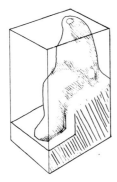

Fig. 17 Developing the figure

Fig. 18 Head based on African
sculpture from cylindrical log
(the remainder of the figure fits
into the same cylinder)
A head drawn on cylindrical
block
B distortion of the drawing
when seen from the side
C head drawn as it should be
seen
D how the head fits in the block

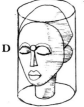

4 Bearing these key points in mind, cut off all corners, getting away from the cuboid feel of the block. If using a maquette (sketch model, p.27), careful observation will show that whole planes at an angle to the square can be developed.

5 As the external shape develops, hollows will begin to form in appropriate places (e.g. between feet, between arms and lap). It should be noted here that hollows must not be made too big to start with. Note the marks of high points on the surface of the block, and avoid the temptation to make, say, the face in proportion, in its present undeveloped state. In the end it will be quite small, and if it is developed in proportion at an early stage, material may be cut away which will eventually be required, and you might have a nick which interferes with the chest, the neck or the chin. It is surprising how relationships change as a sculpture progresses. I have seen a student have to abandon a block of stone altogether through committing herself to the exact size and position of the head of a figure too early in the development.

The golden rule is *never commit yourself until you have to*; *never commit yourself until you are quite sure*.

6 Holes usually come quite late, and only when the degree of development demands it (see figs 22–3). It will be found, as the sculpture develops, that it makes its own demands and that, unless certain material is removed, work cannot proceed. This is the natural evolution of the work, and it is best to let it happen naturally, without forcing and without permitting oneself the luxury of working on a section because that is the most interesting.

Carving from a cylindrical block

Something of the same approach can be used when working on a cylindrical block, such as a length of tree trunk or ivory tusk.

A profile can be drawn on the block from one view, which will indicate volumes that can be cut away. It should be noted, however, that the drawing is valid from one view only, and as soon as the viewpoint is changed the drawing becomes meaningless.

Unless there are large quantities to be removed, blocking-out of this kind is not recommended, as it tends to convert the cylinder into a cuboid form.

It is often useful to draw or paint a profile on the block, work to it from that angle, then make another from a different viewpoint—and work to that. This is a more piecemeal way than front view, side view described for a rectangular block, and will help to retain the roundness of the original block.

Fig. 19 Rough lump with a few corners removed

Carving from a random shape

Pieces of bone, horn and ivory have been carved since prehistoric times, subtly using the form that is already there, amending and shaping it into a sculpture. To dress a random lump of stone into a rectilinear block is mason's work, and, apart from doing so as an exercise or because of cost consideration, is a waste of time for the sculptor. Unless it is a case of squaring-up a base for a sculpture, it is better to make a virtue of the irregular shape and to let it inspire the composition. One sees shapes in a twisted piece of tree trunk or a lump of stone, much as one reads shape in the clouds or the fire.

In the example shown in figs 19–25, choice of form is conditioned partly by the shape of the block and partly by memory of a number of other sculptures carried out on a similar theme. Once the sculpture is visualized within the block, mark major volumes that can be cut away and remove them. Unless the proposed sculpture is very close in form to the shape of the block, it is important that the main masses should be developed as soon as possible. This enables the vision to be maintained and at the same time excludes from the mind detail which should only be developed towards the end. When the broad shape is developed, and the randomness of the block has disappeared, this is the time to re-examine and re-consider the sculpture. Vision is becoming reality. Continue as described previously, marking and cutting away, until doubt is replaced by certainty and the sculpture reaches the finishing stage.

Fig. 20 Form being developed with coarse tools

Fig. 21 Form being developed with coarse tools

Fig. 22 Development includes the use of abrading tools. A hole is drilled through the centre with a hand drill

Fig. 23 Development with chisels (including bullnose chisel), rasp and riffler

Fig. 24 Basic forms completed

Fig. 25 Sculpture ready for removal of the small supporting columns left to give strength while working. Once these are removed, all that remains is the polishing

Relief carving

A relief carving is one that is intended to be looked at from a single viewpoint, rather than from all round, or one that is attached to a background. It is true that some sculptures in the round are so

Fig. 20

Fig. 21

Fig. 22

Fig. 23

Fig. 24

Fig. 25

positioned that they may be looked at from the front only, and that the carving of the back is neglected (for instance, much carving on the exterior of Gothic cathedrals). Here the concept of the whole is in essence a relief, while the individual items are, in fact, carved in the round and placed in position as part of the relief. In fact there is no hard dividing line between the two.

Relief carving may be categorized as high, low, or pierced. While in practice it may not matter what category a relief falls into, it is useful to discuss the nature of relief, from a traditional viewpoint, so that the student is able to control the result and communicate his ideas to the observer.

HIGH RELIEF

This may vary from a figure almost in the round, merely attached to a background, to sculpture verging on low relief. The essential about high relief is that it involves a number of planes—that is to say, the nearest elements are highest and the furthest elements are lowest. They may be clearly distinguishable or one may run into the next, but when designing for high relief the planes must be born in mind.

Generally speaking it is not good practice to have one point higher than all the rest. A number of points so arranged that the eye will carry over them from one to the other maintains the essential flatness of the relief, while the drop from highest planes progressively to lowest expresses the depth.

The action in classical relief tends to be at right-angles to the observer, that is to say, on the plane of the relief. This avoids problems of figures coming out towards the observer and, architecturally, expresses the surface of the building to which the relief is attached. Elements moving from front to back imply space through the wall.

In all relief, whether high or low, the figures tend to be flattened; that is to say, they are not carved as though cut in half. If this is done, it looks as though the figure is, indeed, cut in half by the background. It is usual to squash the figure, so that it is flattened on top and steep at the sides. The background may pass behind the figure or through it, but it will not appear sliced in half.

LOW RELIEF

This is usually on one plane only, and the depth of carving is small, as implied by the name (see figs 28, 30).

The process may come very close to drawing, and the design must be thought out carefully, so that the elements can be arranged on one plane without muddle.

Some ancient sculptors arranged several planes on a low relief.

Fig. 26 Lapith and centaur, south Metope of the Parthenon, about 445 BC. British Museum, London

Fig. 27 Romanesque relief from Chartres Cathedral. This figure is almost in the round, but attached both at back and side. Photo E. Houvet

Here it was usually done by subtly tipping the plane, or dropping the lower plane locally to allow space for the upper one.

Less sophisticatedly, an element superimposed on another was sometimes dropped into a groove.

Here it must be remembered that the sculptor is dealing with a hard material with a fixed surface. A modelled relief is built up and an element can be slightly raised, but when carving, the surface of the block is the limit of height, and everything else has to be cut back. Obviously it is not economic to cut back the whole sculpture to allow one or two minor elements to remain on top. Thought must be given as to how a result can be achieved economically, both in labour and in material.

The method for carving both high and low relief is to draw it on the block, determine the maximum depth, and clear areas back to the background level. This leaves the outline of the relief raised. Levels, where there are more than one, are then developed and the form given to the sculpture.

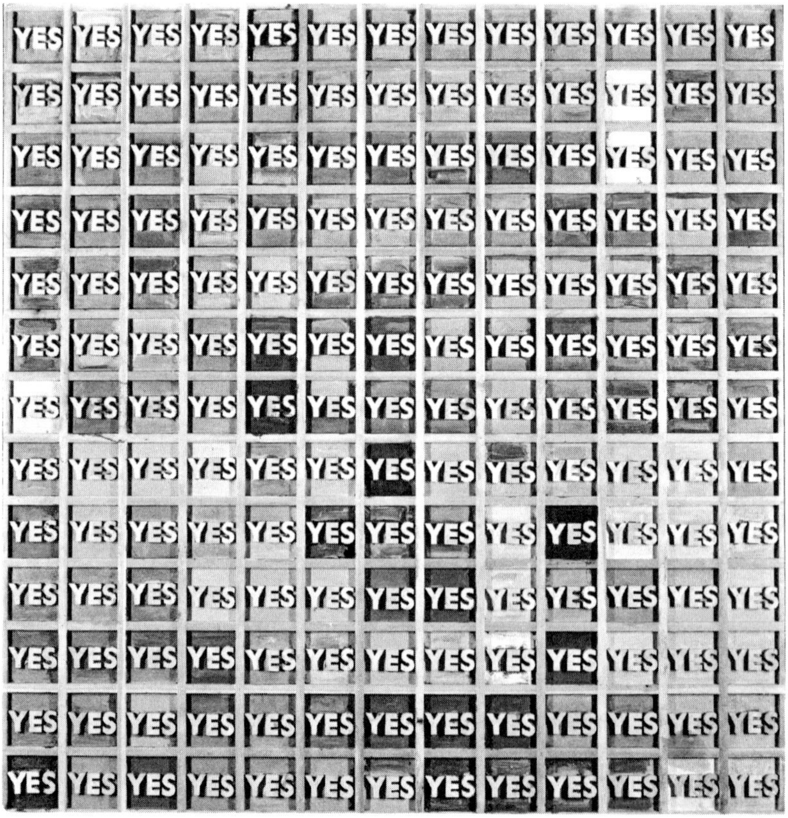

Fig. 28 *Page 1, Penelope* by Joe Tilson. Oil on wood relief, 1969. Marlborough Fine Art (London) Ltd

Fig. 29 Maori door lintel. Pierced relief, wood. Horniman Museum, London

Finally, surface texture and pattern are developed and the appropriate finish given, depending on material used.

PIERCED RELIEF

This may be any scale, from very small to very large. Small, even tiny, pierced relief carvings are often used as jewellery or amulets. These were very common in Ancient Egypt, but have probably been made throughout history. They were, and are usually, made in precious or semi-precious stone, or in ivory, but it is possible to cut them in hard, close-grained wood such as box, rosewood and lignum vitae, or slate and similar stones. Acrylic is another suitable material.

Metal can be worked with tools as well as cast, and brass or aluminium is a suitable material for small work. Silver and gold have been used in the past, but are more often cast and the casting tooled. When making a pierced sculpture, whether relief or in the round, strength is the main technical consideration.

Fragile materials such as concrete building block, or soft stone or wood, where the grain is short (fig. 71), make powerful demands on both the design ability and the technique of the sculptor.

Most stone will break if elements are thin, and the block is jarred during work. Generally, it is wise to carve the outside shape first, then to drill a hole through the centre and carefully enlarge it outwards towards the completed outside shape. Sometimes, where the hole is to be large and takes up much of the sculpture, it may be preferable to drill a large number of holes all the way round the planned hole and carefully join them up, either by sawing or with chisels. Sometimes the sculptor works a hollow on both sides of the sculpture until they meet and then he continues the cutting back process until the hole is completed.

A *miniature pierced relief*: the material must be sufficiently robust to be able to support fine elements: metal, ivory, hard stone, very hard wood, etc. The design should be worked out on paper and transferred to the material.

Drill holes through the pierced elements. A stand drill or an electric drill on a stand attachment is best. Otherwise, fix the

Fig. 30 *St George,* about 1530,
St George Tombland,
Norwich. Low relief, wood.
Photo Arnold Kent

material down firmly and drill with a hand drill, ensuring that the
bit is appropriate to the hardness of the material.

Enlarge the holes with jeweller's saw, coping saw or fret saw,
needle files, rifflers, etc., and work to shape.

B *large relief*: this may simply be an enlargement of the process
described above. Consider the design carefully in terms of size and
of the material used. Ensure that the elements are so arranged and
supported, and of such a thickness, that they will not be over-fragile.

With wood, ensure that any elements cutting across the grain are
not too thin or too long.

C *relief built from several elements*: Gothic tracery is of this order. The
elements were carved individually and then assembled and cemented
together in position.

Large reliefs are sometimes done in this way today, especially in
architectural work. They may be essentially sculptures in the round
grouped in relief form.

D *intaglio*: this is described on p. 85 under plaster. It can be used in
its own right as a decorative element in Perspex, alabaster and
similar materials.

Direct carving

It is possible to take a block of carving material and carve it without
any initial preparation.

Fig. 31 Detail of fig. 32. Note
the simplicity and vigour of
carving, expressing deep
emotional content.
Photo Warburg Institute,
London
Fig. 32 *The Raising of Lazarus,*
twelfth century, Chichester
Cathedral. Photo Warburg
Institute, London

This extremely direct method is used by some sculptors as their
normal method. It can be very stimulating, and can lead to exciting
forms suggested by the block, especially where this is wood.

An African sculptor may have a block of wood standing in his
workshop for months or even years, sometimes observed consciously, often forgotten on the conscious level: one day the contained
form matures in his mind, he takes the wood and carves the sculpture
—quickly, precisely and without error.

Some pieces of wood or stone almost immediately suggest a shape.
Sometimes the artist is unconsciously or consciously looking for a
suitable block to fulfill his idea. In these cases, the minimum of
preparatory work will be necessary and perhaps even none at all.

It is quite common for a sculptor to have no other guide than
drawing on the block itself, even when work of a highly naturalistic
order is done. It demands adequate research in terms of drawing,
and a powerful visual imagination; or well-understood, traditional
forms which are largely repetitive.

Sketch models

Many sculptors work out their ideas first in the form of sketch
models. These have the advantage of enabling major problems of

27

form to be solved, and the initial broad shape to be understood and developed quickly. The chief disadvantage is that the material of the sketch model is different from the carving material, and there is a danger of producing a design which is unsuitable. The sketch model should usually be smaller than the proposed carving, although when doing a portrait head, for example, it may well be the same size.

Clay is the most common medium for developing ideas and working out major forms. For students unaccustomed to working with clay, a description of techniques involved is given in *Starting with Sculpture* by the author.

There is no reason why clay should not be used for sketch models intended for carving, but there are dangers inherent in using it for this purpose. Clay is built up, while carving is a process of cutting away. Therefore the danger is that a modeller's approach will tend to creep into the sketch and, at worst, the sculpture will not be suitable for the material and tools used.

The implications of this are that, while working with clay, the nature of the final material, its strength, and its weakness, the way it is cut, must be born in mind constantly. A sculpture which is reasonable and economic in clay may be very uneconomic in wood or stone, if large volumes have to be removed for the sake of retaining a relatively unimportant element. In other words, it is necessary to design for the final material, and not in terms of clay.

It is possible to carve a block of leather-hard clay, either with a knife or with a gouge, and this may be the best way of using the material for sketch models for carving.

Plaster: as with clay, plaster of paris may be used for sketch modelling. It is perhaps more useful for designing for stone than for wood. Models may be built up on a wire armature using either plaster and scrim, or plaster-impregnated gauze, and then developed by a process of adding and cutting away alternately (see *Starting with Sculpture*).

It also may be cast in a block and then carved with knife or gouge, (see p. 81), which is closer to the final process.

The great advantage of using clay or plaster for initial exploration is that they are quick and cheap to use, and mistakes can be repaired easily.

Soft stone: some sculptors use a soft Bath stone to produce a scale model of a large sculpture in stone. As it is the same material, it will give quite a close approximation, although difference in quality should be borne in mind (see stones p. 79).

Drawing

This is an important part of the sculpture process. Many students are frightened of drawing and have little ability in this direction.

Nevertheless it is a necessary part of the sculptor's vocabulary and should be practised. Traditional attitudes to drawing are often a hindrance to a practical approach. The sculptor is not interested in making pictures. What he needs is an ability to think three-dimensionally, using paper and pencil as tools to aid his thinking.

Very often his drawings may be more diagrams than pictures. But whatever the form, the three-dimensional content is of paramount importance. An object drawn from one view should be redrawn from another angle, and from a higher or a lower viewpoint. This applies either to drawing from an object or from life, or to drawing from imagination. Plenty of practice is required to enable the student to judge proportions, relative sizes and angles, and to discover what is important and what is minor in drawing terms.

Academic drawing is often an arid process lacking any sense of purpose, but drawing with sculpture in mind (or any other specific purpose) becomes meaningful and exciting. A plan and elevation of an object becomes as important as a perspective drawing (see fig. 15). In fact, all means of obtaining a deeper understanding of what is in front of one, or in the mind, is valid.

Drawing is used as a means of stimulating and developing ideas. Things seen or things imagined are put on paper, if possible from several viewpoints. These may lead directly to a carving or to the production of sketch models. Problems may arise in the development of the sketch model which drive the sculptor back to finding a solution on paper, or which spark off new ideas which are best noted on paper. Thus the process is often a movement back and forwards between two-dimensional and three-dimensional media.

An ability to draw plan and elevation is useful to explain to a merchant what is required in terms of material. Sometimes it is economic to have a merchant or dealer cut away parts of the material by machine before starting the sculpture. This is often best described by means of plan and elevation with, perhaps, a perspective drawing (fig. 16).

Fig. 33 Life drawing by student. Three-dimensional analysis

It is also useful for the sculptor himself to be able to work out by these means what major pieces of material can be cut away and where the block should be marked.

Drawing on the block itself is constantly used; first as just described, to indicate where major volumes can be removed, and all the way through the carving process to indicate new profiles, centre lines, etc. Note that these markings are often valid only when observed from one point of view and become meaningless seen from another angle (fig. 18A, B). When they are cut away during the carving process, they should be replaced piecemeal as they disappear.

Fig. 34 Life drawing by student. Three-dimensional analysis

Ivory

Ivory is one of the ancient materials that has been carved from time immemorial. Eskimos carve walrus ivory, Africans of the tropics carve the tusks of elephants. Elephant ivory is carved throughout the Far East. Sailors, especially whalers, carved the teeth of whales. Ivory was carved for ornament and jewellery in ancient times; Gothic carvers made covers for bibles and backs for mirrors. It is carved with infinite subtlety and complexity in India and China. Renaissance craftsmen too made superb carvings in the material.

Sculptors use ivory today, but probably less than in the past, although the trade still thrives in the Far East.

Nevertheless, the material is obtainable from merchants, and the cost is not excessive when compared with, say, bronze casting. Indeed small pieces of scrap ivory can be obtained quite cheaply, which puts the material within the reach of anyone. Ivory may also be obtained from junk shops, secondhand and antique shops—either in the form of tusks and teeth mounted as trophies, or already made into articles such as billiard balls, paper knives, etc.

Fig. 35 *Assault on the House of Egil the Archer*. Whalebone relief, Frankish, about seventh to eight century. British Museum, London

Fig. 36 Ivory Salt. Benin, Nigeria (carved to Portuguese commission), sixteenth century. British Museum, London

Types

Elephant ivory is the most usual kind, and the most readily obtainable. Most Indian ivory is used in the Far East, so the ivory usually obtainable is African. This is not so white as Indian ivory, having a bluer tinge. The tusks of the elephants from the forests of Central Africa are shorter, straighter and harder than the mighty, curved tusks we see on the elephants from the grasslands of Central and East Africa. The lower, wider part of the tusk that attaches to the animal is hollow, the upper part being solid. The lower part is covered with hard enamel which has to be removed before this part of the tusk can be used for carving. It is similar in colour to the ivory but runs longitudinally in ridges along the tusk and is, therefore, easily identifiable. It is between one and two millimetres in thickness.

Hippopotamus tooth is whiter than tusk and is harder. Its cost is that of scrap elephant ivory, making it very economical. The whole front of the tooth is covered with hard enamel, which must be removed. The hollow in a hippopotamus tooth is quite deep, and continues right through the tooth to the tip, in the form of a dark line.

Numbers of other teeth or tusks have been carved, including those of some kinds of whales, but elephant and hippopotamus are those most generally used. Other types vary in their qualities, but not a great deal. It is mainly a question of availability and appropriate shape and size that governs the carveability of a tooth—that and the amount of enamel that has to be removed before carving starts.

Tools

Saw—hacksaw, with hard blade, for major cutting, coping saw and jeweller's saw for cutting out shapes.
Gouges—either woodcarver's or engraver's.
Files—coarse and medium, half round and round, needle files for fine work.
Rifflers—shaped files.
Twist drill.
Knife—(X-acto or Stanley knife), graver, etc.
Electric sander.
Abrasives.

Equipment

Bench—heavy table will do.
Vice—engineer's vice or carpenter's vice.
Hand-vice—for holding when doing fine work.
Chops—woodcarver's chops (see p. 45).

Working

Sawing: large cuts can be made with a hacksaw. Note that blades will be blunted very quickly, and should be changed regularly. Lubricate cuts with water during sawing.

Smaller cuts, such as fretting out a shape, are made with a coping saw or jeweller's saw. If an enclosed shape is to be cut out, drill through it, thread the saw blade through the hole, fix in the saw and cut out.

Gouges must be sharp and are usually pushed with the hand only, not used with a mallet. A good deal of carving is possible with gouge or chisel, and traditionally sailors carved with a jack-knife. The latter can be dangerous for anyone unpractised in carving with a knife. Precautions are necessary when using chisel or gouge: fix the carving firmly in a vice and keep hands behind the tool. Do not carve with chisel or gouge when holding the sculpture in the hand (see also woodcarving p. 50).

In ivory carving a lot of work is done with abrading tools—files and rifflers. This is because ivory carvings tend to be small and delicate, and because the nature of the material seems to demand this treatment. The beauty of the material is brought out by smoothing and polishing. It has a subtle figuring which varies from one type to another, which may not be apparent unless polished.

Once the initial cutting out has been done, a half-round or round file and rifflers can be used for much of the work. A number of different shapes and sizes of rifflers is an advantage. Needle files are useful too. They are particularly useful if the sculpture is in the form of a pierced relief. Ivory has considerable strength and can be worked in very fine sections, but for this fine tools are necessary. These will probably consist of a jeweller's saw, small rifflers and needle files, and abrasive paper twisted into cones or glued to slivers of wood (see below). Blades such as a Stanley knife or X-acto knife are also useful both for carving and for smoothing.

Polishing

Initial polishing can be done with sandpaper or medium grades of wet-or-dry, moving on to fine as polishing proceeds—used first dry, then wet. Corners may be difficult on a fine carving, and will require patience and ingenuity. Wet-or-dry carborundum paper wrapped round small sticks, or emery cloth glued to pieces of wood, can be utilized. How the carving is polished will depend on the nature of the sculpture. It is easy to take off all hard edges and to leave a generally rounded and smooth appearance, but one of the qualities to consider when carving is the contrast between hard line and soft form. Pay attention to this, and beware of rounding everything off indiscriminately.

Final polish is given with abrasive powder. Pumice powder used wet with a small, stiff brush, followed by a household cleansing powder such as Vim, or a similar fine abrasive powder, will give a good polish on ivory. Some household cleansers contain bleach, which is not desirable. This part of the process is best done over a sink where the powder can be washed off regularly with cold or warm (not hot) water.

Finally polish the sculpture with a soft cloth. The harder it is rubbed, the better will be the polish. Beware of breaking delicate elements—if the sculpture is small and flat, it should be put on a flat surface and rubbed.

Wood

Fig. 37 Cross section of log, showing annual rings

Wood is composed of longitudinal bundles of fibres, and this is the major characteristic which affects its manipulation. If it were not so, a tree would not be able to support its own weight. One only has to compare the longitudinal strength of a narrow piece of chipboard or hardboard (where the fibrous structure of the wood has been destroyed by shredding or pulping) with a strip of wood of similar dimensions to see what an important factor in terms of strength this is.

Another important characteristic of wood is its annual growth. A tree grows thicker as it grows taller. When a tree is cut down, the concentric rings on the cut end demonstrate its age. One ring equals one year's growth, and the age of a felled tree can be determined easily by this means. During the growing period growth is fast, indicated by a wide lightish ring, and towards the rest period, as growth slows, the ring becomes darker and denser. Variations in growth rate can be noted by the relative width of these rings: a band of wide rings denotes a series of good growing years and a band of narrow ones the reverse. Generally speaking, fast-growing trees produce softer wood than slow-growing ones.

There is a tendency for trees to grow with a spiral twist, which also increases their resistance to wind, etc. If one stands beneath a tall tree and looks up, both the markings on the bark and the way branches grow out from the trunk will indicate this. Usually it is not an important factor, unless very long pieces of wood are used.

A tree is fed mainly by liquid (sap) containing nutrients passing up the fibres. As it grows, the cells making up the inner annual rings clog up with a gummy material, cease to function as part of the feeding system and become the tree's support. The outer rings continue to pass food up to the branches, twigs and leaves.

The inner part, which is often darker in colour, is called the heartwood; the outer, sap-bearing wood is called sapwood. This latter part of the tree is usually soft and not suitable for use, although there are exceptions, where sapwood is as hard as the heartwood.

Grain

The nature of a tree's growth has been described above. The trunk

35

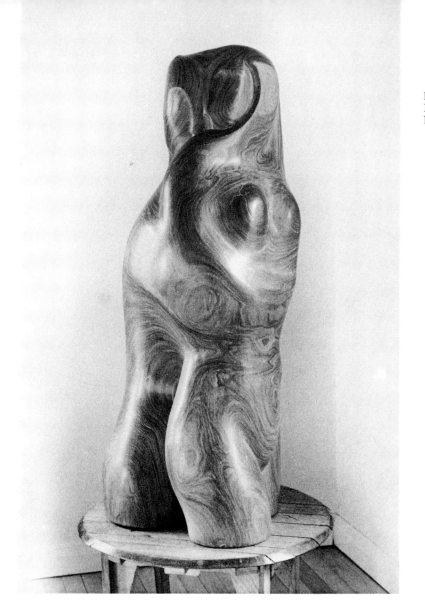

Fig. 38 *Human bondage* by
Duncan Johnston. Lignum vitae.
Photo Bernard Alfieri

consists of longitudinal bundles of fibres, growing in concentric
rings. When the tree is cut into planks or baulks, these fibres are called
the *grain*. The grain in the block to be carved will depend on how the
tree has been cut up. As the wood dries the shrinkage will be uneven,
depending on the grain, so the flat boards or baulks will tend to
curve or distort.

Appearance

There is great variety of colour in wood, from off-white to red and
black. It may also be dramatically or subtly striped and variegated.

Fig. 39 Wood sculpture by
Peter Startup. The sculpture is
built from a number of elements

Sculptors can make use of these qualities, emphasizing them by careful smoothing and polishing. In the past carvers often gessoed and painted a sculpture, so that the wood itself was completely covered and the only criteria for choice were quality for working and availability.

The most strongly striped of the woods are the softwoods. Note here that the term 'softwood' refers to the coniferous or cone-bearing trees, while 'hardwood' refers to the deciduous or broad-leaved trees.

The coniferous woods often show the wide band as a light strip while the narrow band is dark—often red or brown. Many hardwoods show the grain clearly, but it is usually more as a change of texture and less as a change of colour.

The second factor which makes for variety in colour is the difference between sapwood and heartwood. Often the heartwood is darker than the sapwood, sometimes dramatically so. Where both are strong and useful for carving, the change of colour can give a piebald effect to the sculpture.

Finally, note that the surface of wood tends to darken or to become more yellow when exposed to the light. It can be quite startling, for example, to cut into a piece of mahogany that has been left for a few days in the light and to see how pink the new cut is.

The classification of hardwood and softwood has been noted above. It must be appreciated that this does not refer to the hardness, although generally speaking softwoods are soft. But pitch pine and yew are quite hard, whereas lime is soft, so it will be seen that the terms are only a generalization. So woods can be classified as soft or hard (and perhaps there should be a third classification of medium-hard), but an equally important classification is close-grained or open-grained.

Generally speaking, a close-grained wood is tough, and where this is combined with hardness (as in beech or ebony), the wood becomes difficult to carve. But lime, while tough, is soft, which means that so long as the gouge is sharp, fine carving can be done and sharp edges across the grain will not crumble (for *across* the grain see fig. 59A).

Open-grained woods may be hard, but are not so tough, and hence are more easily cut. It is not possible to do such fine work with the open-grained woods as with close-grained.

Weight has nothing to do with this quality: lime is light, beech is medium, and ebony is heavy; and all are close-grained.

Knots, which develop at the centre of trunks and branches, are hard, sometimes very hard and brittle, and will take the edge off a woodcarving tool. They may have to be filed, sawn or even chipped off.

38

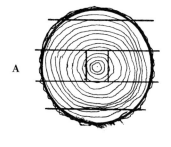

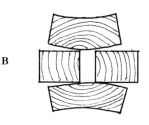

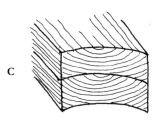

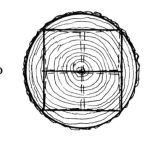

Fig. 40 Effect of drying-out of timber
A trunk sawn up
B warping, due to drying
C showing direction of grain when gluing two planks
D distortion in square-cut baulks due to drying. Note that timber also shrinks when drying

Preparation and seasoning

Most wood bought from merchants is kiln-dried and not completely seasoned, and so it is best kept for some time before using if possible. Seasoning is the process of drying-out the sap and natural moisture in the wood. The longer it is kept before use, the better will it be seasoned. It will shrink during this process.

If you cut down a tree yourself or obtain wood from someone who has, the felling should be done during the rest season (i.e. winter) when sap is not flowing in the tree.

Cut the log into suitable lengths, strip the bark, and paint the exposed ends. This is done to prevent sap drying out of the ends too quickly, otherwise splits will form which tend to continue a long way down the log. It is almost impossible to prevent very sappy wood from splitting.

The lengths of wood should be stored under cover, but in such a position that air can circulate freely round them. They should be kept out of direct sun and artificial heat. Seasoning by this method is a slow process. A rule of thumb is one year for each inch of thickness.

Good, well-seasoned pieces of wood may be obtained from old furniture. Wood found on beaches, in estuaries and rivers is often well-seasoned. It may have been drifting for some time (its appearance will tell whether or not it is still green) and water is a good seasoning agent.

It should be dried carefully and naturally. The same goes for wood picked up in fields and woods.

Tools

Chisel—has a straight edge.
Gouge—has a curved edge.
Mallet—cylindrical (not carpenter's).
Rasp file, riffler, Surform.
Cabinet scraper (shaped if necessary).
Abrasives.
Carpentry tools.

TYPES OF CHISELS AND GOUGES
There are a number of different kinds of woodcarving gouge which have evolved for special purposes. They vary in width from 1 mm. (1/32 in.) to 25 mm. (1 in.). In general, however, three or four types are of importance. Straight chisels and gouges have their sides parallel. If of 19 mm. ($\frac{3}{4}$ in.) or more, they are usually supplied in fishtail (i.e. the sides are not parallel but widen towards the blade).

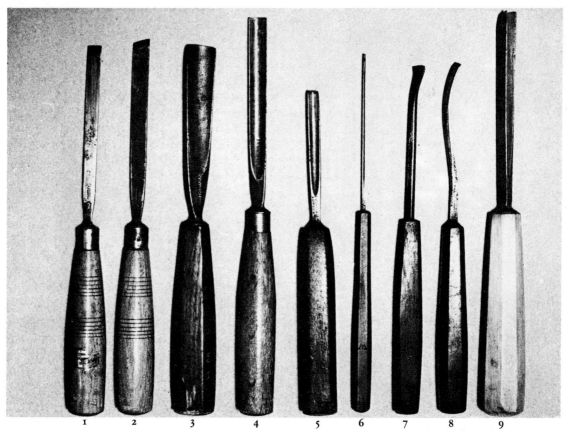

1	2	3	4	5	6	7	8	9

Bent chisels and gouges have the shank bent, so that deep and awkward areas can be worked.

Spades are also bent, but the whole shank is curved.

The sculptor can usually do with a fairly simple range, and designing should be thought of in terms of simple cuts. Chisels and gouges are number-coded for easy reference. The number relates to the deepness of the gouge, and not to its width.

Fig. 41 Tools for wood carving: **1, 2** chisels. **3, 4** gouges. **5** fluter. **6** veiner. **7** bent. **8** spade. **9** parting tool or V-tool

Straight and Fishtail

No. 1—a chisel (i.e. a tool with a straight edge), but unlike a carpenter's chisel, sharpened on both sides.

No. 2—similar to No. 1, but with the cutting edge bevelled.

Nos 3–9—gouges that are an arc of a circle, No. 3 being very shallow—almost flat—and No. 9 being a semi-circle.

Nos 10, 11—U-shaped gouges, No. 11 being deeper than No. 10. No. 10 are known as fluters and No. 11 as veiners.

Nos 39–41—V-tools or parting tools.

Bent:

Nos 21–32—these start flat, and get deeper as the number increases, as with straight and fishtail.

Nos 43–44—parting tools.

MALLET

A carver's mallet is traditionally cylindrical. This type has been found in Ancient Egyptian tombs, and paintings of medieval craftsmen show examples almost identical with those we use today. This is because the ideal shape was discovered at a very early stage, and it has never been bettered. The shape is natural, as it comes easily from the round section of a branch or small tree trunk; and as it is cylindrical, unlike a hammer or a carpenter's mallet, it has no specific striking face.

The heavier the wood, the smaller the mallet can be. Lignum vitae, a very heavy, dense wood is most usually used today, but beech and hickory are also employed.

Use as heavy a mallet as you can handle, for a big mallet makes roughing-out much quicker and easier. It is a good idea to have a second, lighter mallet for delicate work.

FIXING HANDLES

In the past woodcarvers usually made their own handles for their chisels and gouges. Often pieces of hardwood were collected and fine handles, usually octagonal, were tailored to the individual chisel.

Nowadays it is more common to buy hardwood handles, either round, with a brass ferrule, or octagonal. They are usually drilled to take the handle, but this hole is only a starter, and if the handle is knocked direct on to the gouge, it will almost certainly split.

Fix the gouge vertically in a vice, taking care not to damage the blade, tang (the spike that goes into the handle) uppermost. Place the handle over the tang and tap lightly with a mallet. Twist the handle, tap, twist again and continue until it is almost home. Then one or two light taps will fix the handle firmly.

The chisel or gouge is now ready for its initial sharpening. Nowadays, a gouge, when bought new, has been cast rather than wrought, and its cutting edge has been roughly ground. Much work is required to get it to a good enough condition for carving, but it is essential that it should be done properly.

The edge of a woodcarving gouge is sharpened to a different angle from that of a carpenter's chisel and, because a finer edge is required, it is usually sharpened on both sides. This is described in detail on p. 47.

ABRADING AND SMOOTHING TOOLS

Rasp is the chief abrading tool. It is a kind of file covered with oval teeth, which tear the wood. It can be obtained from very coarse to fine. I find the very coarse most useful, although some care has to be taken in using it, as it may tear the grain more deeply than you want

Fig. 42

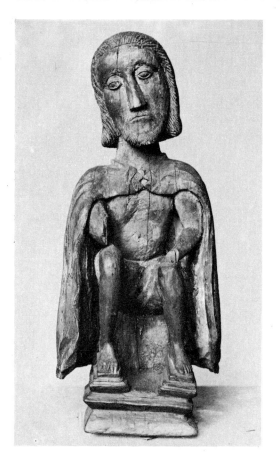

Fig. 43

Fig. 45

Fig. 44

Fig. 42 *Pieta*, Polish. Polychrome wood. Photo Stefan Deptuszenski

Fig. 43 *Christ*, Polish. Lime wood. Photo Stefan Deptuszenski

Fig. 44 Tomb effigy, Fersfield, Norfolk. Polychrome wood

Fig. 45 *The Little Man*, St Albans Abbey. Polychrome wood. Photo Eric Gowlland

if used without caution. Except on very soft wood, other tools do the work of fine rasps as well or better than the rasp itself.

Files may be used for smoothing the work after rasping.

Dreadnought is a kind of file with a series of bars across it, which acts rather like a plane. It is used with the grain, or half with—half across, and removes quite a lot of wood while refining and smoothing at the same time.

Surform has largely superseded the dreadnought and, to some extent, the rasp, although it has to be used with caution. Surform is a trade name, and is the original of a family of tools consisting of a pierced blade held in a frame. It works in much the same way as a vegetable grater. The frame can be obtained in a number of forms to suit individual requirements, and the blades can be either curved or flat. There is also a rat-tail version (i.e. a long narrow cylinder).

The tool acts like a combination of plane and file. It tends to remove wood very rapidly, and herein lies its danger. It is easy to take off too much and leave a hollow or a flat plane where a convex is required. Used carefully it is a very useful tool. It does not smooth the wood perfectly, but leaves numerous flattened ridges which have to be removed by other means.

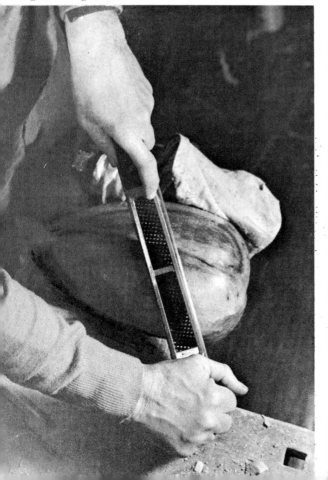

Fig. 46 Using Surform

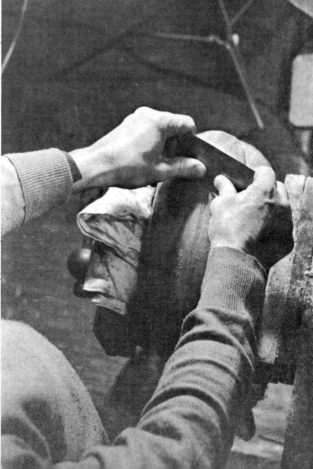

Fig. 47 Using cabinet scraper

Riffler is a small, shaped rasp. It consists of a short metal rod with a differently shaped rasp on either end. It can be obtained in a variety of shapes and sizes, and is invaluable for working difficult corners and hollows.

Scraper is a rectangle of tensile steel. A burr is put on the edge by dragging a piece of hard steel along it, then the surface of the wood can be scraped smooth with it. It is held firmly with both hands at an angle of about 60° to the surface of the wood and dragged over the surface. When it blunts, the edge is resharpened, again by dragging hard steel along it. Scrapers can be made to a suitable shape for concave surfaces. Mark out the required shape on the scraper and trim with snips (metal shears) or a guillotine, then file to shape. Scrapers are obtained in varying dimensions and thicknesses. If too thick, they are difficult to shape (fig. 47).

ABRASIVE PAPERS

Sandpaper or glasspaper is usually used for final smoothing. It can be obtained in varying grades, from very coarse to very fine. Garnet paper is similar. It costs more but lasts much longer.

If possible, wrap the paper round a block of wood, cork or expanded polystyrene. This saves wear and tear on the fingers.

It is often necessary to use it with the fingers however, in which case small pieces of paper should be torn off the sheet and used until worn. Very fine paper may be used for final finishing, but remember that as the paper wears it becomes finer, so worn pieces of medium may in fact be found to be fine enough.

Work *with* the grain, especially when finishing. Scratches which may be difficult to remove will be made if glasspapering is done across the grain.

The final glasspapering of a sculpture is often a tedious business. It is better to work at a small area and get that quite smooth, then to move on to the next. Hard pressure is required, and it is difficult to keep it up on a large area. It is also more encouraging to see an area come up smooth and clean quickly, even though it is small. Working on a large area which only improves slowly can be most disheartening.

Equipment

Bench.
Vice or chops.
G-clamp.
Oilstone.
Slipstone (slip).
Strop.

BENCH

A purpose-built carver's bench is best. It has a heavy top, at least 50 mm. (2 ins) thick, preferably 65–70 mm. (2½–3 ins). There is usually a trough at the back of the bench to hold tools, pieces of wood, etc. (a doubtful benefit). Although purpose-built benches usually have hardwood tops, a softwood top is also satisfactory. To build a bench, use 75 mm. × 50 mm. (3 × 2 in.) timber, half-lapped and bolted for the frame. Two widths of timber 250 mm. (10 in.) or wider, and at least 50 mm. (2 ins) thick should be used for the top. Sometimes suitable, well-dried timber can be obtained from a demolition site.

A heavy old-fashioned kitchen table may also be used, though the top will require reinforcing, and as it is normally too low for comfortable work, it will have to be blocked up. Height will depend on height of the user but 840 mm. (33 ins) is a minimum.

HOLDING METHODS

The bench should be fitted with a carpenter's vice and, preferably, an end vice, which is included in a purpose-built bench. It consists of a screw on one end of the bench, working a block set within the dimension of the bench top. A piece of wood can be held between the block and the bench, or on the surface of the bench between a peg fitted into an appropriate hole and a similar one on the vice (fig. 48).

Another very useful vice is a carver's chop. It consists of a vice with wood jaws lined with cork and leather, and is fixed to the top of the bench by a bolt. It will hold irregular shapes firmly (figs 48–9).

Wood can be held on the bench or on a block to be held in the vice by means of a bench screw. A hole is drilled in the base of the piece to be carved and the bench screw is screwed into it. It is passed through the bench top or through a block and tightened up underneath with a wing nut (fig. 51A).

A relief may be held with the end-vice, with bench clips, or, if of simple shape, by means of battens (wood strips) nailed to the bench round the edge of the wood. Larger sculptures can be rested in the chops with one end on the bench. A pad of several clean sacks or layers of thick material, perhaps supported with wood wedges, will take up the shape of an awkward piece of wood, which can also be held with G-clamps.

Sharpening

A considerable percentage of a woodcarver's time is spent in sharpening his chisels. They are usually kept literally razor sharp, and time spent on this is more than saved by ease of work.

Fig. 48 Bench, showing vice and chops

Fig. 49 Chops

Fig. 50 Board for oilstones and slips

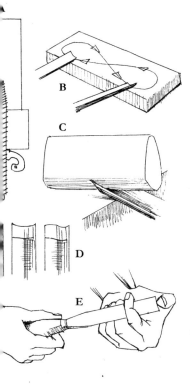

Fig. 51
A benchscrew showing log fixed to a block to be held in the vice
B sharpening a gouge—gouge is rocked as it makes figure-of-eight movement
C sharpening inside of gouge with slip
D *left* correctly-sharpened gouge; *middle, right* incorrectly-sharpened gouge
E testing sharpness of gouge

OILSTONES

These are of two kinds, artificial and natural.

Artificial oilstones are made in a number of grades, usually three: coarse, medium and fine. One each of these stones is best, although combined stones can be bought, medium on one side and fine on the other. They are usually approximately 150–200 mm. long by 50 mm. wide. Natural stones are of two kinds: Washita stones are a little finer than a fine artificial stone. Arkansas stone is very hard and fine. It cuts away the metal very slowly, giving a fine, almost burnished edge. It is relatively expensive, and because of cost is usually smaller than the usual oilstone. Natural stones replace the fine grade of artificial stone.

A box is often made to hold the stone firmly, in which case it is usually fixed in with putty. A good idea is to make a special board for holding sharpening equipment. Squares of batten (wood strip) will stop the oilstone from sliding, and are useful if a stone is double-sided and has to be reversed.

SLIPSTONES

These consist of shaped strips of stone, artificial or natural, shaped to fit the insides of gouges (fig. 51C).

Both natural and artificial stones are bought shaped, but sometimes rough scraps of natural stone—particularly arkansas stone—can be purchased.

It is often convenient to have the curve on the slipstone tapered, so that one slip may sharpen a number of gouges.

Shaping of slips is done with a grinder and/or emery cloth, or wet-or-dry carborundum paper.

Initial sharpening of a new gouge is done on a coarse oilstone (nowadays an artificial stone such as an indiastone is mostly used).

A carpenter's chisel is sharpened by holding the chisel at the appropriate angle and moving it backwards and forwards on the stone. A gouge, especially a carving gouge, needs different treatment.
1 See that the oilstone (coarse or medium) is held firmly (fig. 50). Put on a few drops of a thin lubrication oil (e.g. 3 in 1 oil).
2 Holding the gouge at an angle of approx. 15° to the horizontal, move the gouge sideways along the stone in the form of a figure of eight, at the same time rocking it from side to side (fig. 51B). Press the blade of the gouge lightly but firmly onto the stone with the fingers of the left hand.

Take care to grind the blade evenly; quite often too much weight is given on the centre of the stroke, when the sharpened chisel develops ears on the corners, or at one end of the stroke, when the edge becomes wavy (fig. 51D).

As the initial grinding carried out at the factory may be very uneven, care must be taken and constant observation kept to see that thin parts of the edge are not over-ground. This may be obviated by noting where the blade is extra thick, and pressing more heavily where these points are in contact with the stone during the figure-of-eight movement, lightening the weight where the edge is thin. Wipe off dirty oil with cotton waste, a piece of rag or a tissue.

3 When the worst of the rough sharpening is done, the inside of the gouge must be sharpened. This is done with a slip. Ideally each gouge should have an appropriate slipstone of an equal arc. It is rarely possible however, unless there is one that fits exactly, so the slip-stone of next smaller radius to the gouge should be used.

Hold the gouge at an angle against the edge of the bench, blade up. Lubricate the slip with a drop of thin oil or paraffin, and sharpen the inside of the blade at an angle of approx 15° evenly along its inside edge. If it is a large gouge, and has not been sharpened previously, an artificial stone may be used; but generally speaking a washita slip is used at first (fig. 51C).

4 Continue sharpening the outside edge, first with a fine artificial stone and then, preferably, with a natural stone (usually a washita).

5 Alternatively sharpen the inside and outside of the gouge until a fine edge is achieved. This is checked in two ways:

A Move the gouge so that the light strikes the edge. Any over-thick part will show up as a silver line.

B Hold the chisel firmly in the right hand. Rest the fingers of the left hand firmly on the blade and slide the ball of the left thumb very lightly along the edge (fig. 51E). The blade should just nick the skin very slightly as it moves along the edge. If done properly, no damage is done to the thumb, although it takes a certain amount of nerve to do it for the first time. The thumb should not be dragged *across* the blade as is common practice. Doing this tells one nothing, but may damage the edge.

6 If an arkansas slip or stone is available, finish the sharpening with this.

7 Despite all the sharpening, and however fine the stones, a thin wire will be left on the edge of the blade. This is removed with a leather strop (i.e. a thick leather strap) (fig. 52).

Place the gouge on the strop and draw it towards you, rocking it from left to right as you do so, so that the whole edge of the gouge is treated. Do this a number of times. Bend a piece of strop into an appropriate curve, and place the inside of the gouge upon it. Draw it towards you several times, along the leather. The gouge should now be ready for use.

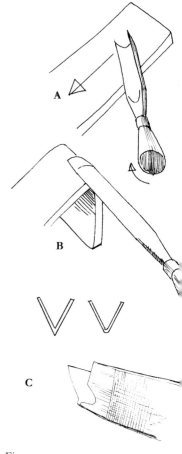

Fig. 52
A stropping outside of gouge
B stropping inside of gouge
C sharpening parting tool: *left* wrong, *middle* right, *right* result of correct sharpening

MAINTENANCE

It will be necessary to strop the gouge every five or ten minutes during use, depending on the wood being worked and the type of work done. Occasionally it should be touched up with a fine slip and oilstone.

A DAMAGED GOUGE

If the edge of a gouge has been chipped, the whole edge must be ground down vertically until the chip has completely disappeared, and then sharpening restarted as described above.

It is unwise to use an electric grinder, and if one is used, great care must be taken not to burn the tool. Excessive heat takes the temper out of the steel, which becomes soft and useless. A coarse oilstone is slower but safer.

PARTING TOOL

The sharpening of this tool is not easy. It is not possible to sharpen both inside and outside to a sharp V; if it is attempted, one of the sides of the V is invariably worn away (fig. 52C).

Fig. 53 Tools in their permanent rack

In practice the bottom of the V is sharpened to a small radius, the only way of getting a fine edge all round.

Fig. 54 Tools in felt tool-roll for transporting

BENT TOOL

As this gouge may be cup-shaped, sharpening the inside is most easily done with a special tool. It can be made by carving a piece of wood to a dome-shape, the same as the inside of the gouge, and smearing it with carborundum paste. It is also possible to grind the corner of a slip to fit inside the cup.

STORING GOUGES

When not being used during work, gouges should be laid on the bench, edge towards you, so that the edge will not be damaged by impact with other tools, and so that the required tool can be seen easily.

They should be stored either in a rack (fig. 53) or on a wood tray, and for transport a felt roll should be made. The handles are stuck into pockets and the blades lie between the handles of the gouges opposite. Make the roll wide enough that blades do not stick out of the end when it is rolled up (fig. 54).

PRECAUTIONS

Gouges, being razor-sharp, are potentially dangerous if misused, but with proper precautions they are quite safe. The rule is: always fix your work down when using chisel or gouge. Keep hands *behind* the blade. Do not hold work in the hand.

Fig. 55 Carving by John
Spielman. Beech

Fig. 56 *Flower* by Robert
Dawson. Greenheart

Working wood

The fibrous structure of wood has been discussed on p. 35. The way wood is worked is governed by this structure. The direction of the fibre is known as the grain.

Sawing

Wood may be sawn in any direction, but when sawing *with* (i.e. along) the grain, a saw with large teeth set to give a wide cut is necessary, otherwise the blade jams between the fibres. Cutting *across* the grain demands a saw with smaller teeth, making a finer cut, as a big one will tear the fibres too much. The wood to be sawn should be fixed firmly in a suitable position. The knuckle of the left thumb is used to guide the saw when beginning to cut (fig. 58). Rest the hand on the wood and hold the thumb so that the saw is steadied by it. The shoulder should be lined up with the saw to give the direction of the cut (fig. 57). Hold the saw quite loosely. If the hand is clenched and the muscles tightened, the saw will almost certainly drift off the line, and it will be very difficult to bring it back. With the saw held loosely, it is much easier to follow the line, and to bring the saw back when it strays.

Fig. 57 Shoulder lined up with saw

Fig. 58 Thumb used to guide saw when starting

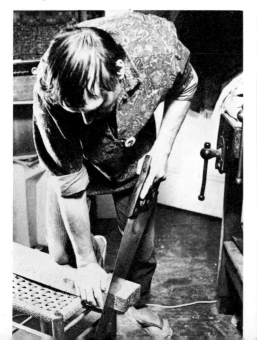

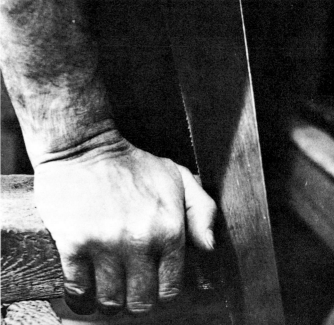

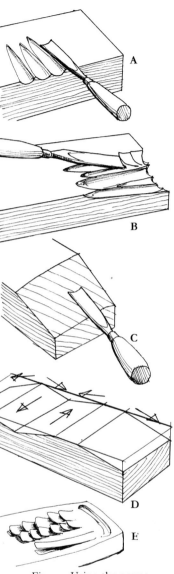

Gouge

A sharp gouge or chisel will cut across the grain cleanly, unless the wood is very soft indeed. If it is not sharp, the gouge will tend to tear the wood.

When working along the grain it is important to cut with the grain and not against it (fig. 59B). This means that one is cutting obliquely across the fibres, as when sharpening a pencil. If the gouge is worked against the grain, it will tend to get jammed in between the fibres and may well either split off a piece of wood or break a piece out of the cutting edge of the gouge (fig. 59C).

If a gouge is jammed in the wood, it should be left there and the wood around it cut away carefully with another gouge until it can be removed without damage.

When clearing a flat area, first make a cut with the gouge near the line marking the extent of the area to be cleared, or else make a channel with a fluter or a parting tool. Then work back away from this cut, taking out a fairly small chip each time (fig. 59E). If the initial cut is not made, the wood may split beyond the point desired. If the cuts are too far apart in an attempt to take out too big chips, the gouge may jam in the wood. A deep gouge should be used, (say a No. 8), so that the ears do not get buried.

The row of chips will either flip out themselves as the next cut is made, or else a second row of cuts are made in the opposite direction to remove them. Do not dig out chips with the gouge—the edge is sure to be damaged.

Generally speaking, work starts with a large gouge, often a fairly deep one. Making a hollow or hole usually requires a high number—say a No. 8 or No. 7, whereas making a convex shape may best be done with a low number, say a No. 5 or No. 4.

When it comes to fining down a surface, a gouge as close as possible to the curve required is used. Convex surfaces are done with a low number—No. 4 or No. 3.

A flat surface is made with a No. 3, not a No. 1 as might be expected. A No. 3 has a very shallow curve, the corners having enough lift to avoid digging into the surface (which will invariably happen if a No. 1 is used for this purpose).

No. 1 is used for making straight cuts, as with a carpenter's chisel, and a No. 2 similarly. The bevel on the latter makes it very useful for cleaning sharp corners.

Carving a sculpture in the round

1 Draw the proposed sculpture on one surface of the wood. If the wood has square faces this is simple; if it is curved—say a piece of

Fig. 59 Using the gouge
A working across the grain
B working *with* the grain—correct
C working *against* the grain—incorrect
D directions in which a block may be worked, either with or across the grain
E channel cut to stop wood from splitting off too far

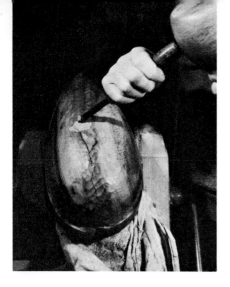

Figs 60–64 Developing the form with gouges. As the sculpture develops, it is moved from the carpenter's vice to the chops, which have soft jaws and hold the rounded form more easily

Fig. 60 Using the gouge (left-handed)

Fig. 61 Carving method: shape marked out with charcoal and corners sawn off. Note how the design is arranged to allow for a bad split in the wood

Fig. 65 Some work done with rasp and Surform, but gouge still used. Note the clay sketch model

Fig. 66 Sculpture ready for smoothing with scrapers, glasspaper, etc.

Fig. 60

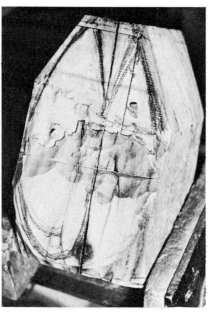

Fig. 61

Fig. 62

Fig. 63

Fig. 64

Fig. 65

Fig. 66

tree trunk—it is more difficult and care must be taken that points are located properly (see p. 19).

2 Decide which pieces can be cut away right across the block and mark them, leaving a little spare to allow for adjustment in the final figure. Saw them off, or alternatively cut them off with a gouge of suitable size (see p. 53).

3 Redraw the figure on the block from another angle, and repeat the process. It may be practical to make the second marking at 90° to the first, but not necessarily so, depending on the form of the sculpture.

4 Note any further big planes which can be cut away, mark them and remove them. If a sketch model is used, a flat plane—a piece of card, a scraper or a rule—can be held against the model and, visualizing the block around it, determine which are the big masses that can be removed quickly. If starting with a square block, ensure that the squareness disappears as soon as possible. This means determining planes which are not at 90° to each other. Once the first few planes have been created, fresh ones at 45° or some other angle are made, so that soon the sculpture develops a rounder feeling.

5 Develop the sculpture, using as large gouges as possible. When necessary, start a hollow from one known high point to another, slowly deepening the hollow and only committing yourself irrevocably when you are quite sure of its size and location. Do not create undercuts until it is absolutely necessary. Proportions change surprisingly as the sculpture fines down; positioning of important points can be deceptive and it is possible, when approaching the final form, to find that material is needed in a place from which it has already been taken away. Remember that wood once removed cannot be replaced.

6 Keep junctions of planes clean. Hairy and ragged junctions are unpleasant. When the time comes to work them, use a No. 1 or appropriate gouge if they are to be sharp. Very often it is not necessary to have a sharp junction, however, and a fluter can be used, giving a smooth transition from one plane to the next.

7 If a chisel finish is intended, work the surface carefully with very sharp gouges. The surface will consist of many little planes (fig. 1).

If a smooth finish is intended (fig. 56), continue with gouges and chisels until the form is as nearly complete as possible, then smooth, using first rasps and/or Surform, then a cabinet scraper (shaped if necessary) and finally fine glasspaper. Some developing of forms is often done with the rasp, but do not depend on it too much: most work should be done with gouges.

Note: Keep the sculpture clean. Towards the end, wrap the work in a clean cloth, exposing only the part being worked.

Mending and patching

Any piece of wood knocked off the block by accident should be replaced immediately. Glue and cramp it in position until set, then continue to work over it in the normal way.

Wood is always liable to move and cracks to appear. I have seen this happen in a piece of oak more than three hundred years old, taken from one of the guild halls destroyed in the bombing of London in 1940. When a piece was cut out of the beam, cracks developed, due to the change of tensions. This will always tend to happen when conditions change: a new set of tensions and stresses come into play and a new balance has to be achieved within the wood.

Cracks or 'shakes' may be caused during growing or felling of the tree, and will appear when wood is being seasoned, due to the shrinkage that takes place during the process, especially if it is not done properly (see p. 39).

Changes of temperature and humidity will cause the wood to open. Central heating is a big problem for the sculptor in wood, where the atmosphere is usually warm and dry. This causes excessive shrinking, twisting, and often cracking. Wood should be introduced to these conditions gradually if possible.

Inevitably there will often be patching of splits and cracks to do. Large splits are filled by making wedges of a suitable similar piece of wood, with the grain going in the same direction as that of the sculpture. The split is cleared of odd fibres if necessary, and the wedges painted with glue and tapped lightly but firmly into place. They should stand proud and the surplus be worked off when the glue has set.

Small faults and cracks, or awkward-shaped holes, are filled with plastic wood—dust from glasspapering the wood of the sculpture is mixed with glue to make a thick paste (a cellulose glue such as Durofix is best, but a white glue will do). This is forced into the fault and left standing proud, to be worked off with glasspaper or gouge when it has thoroughly set. Matching of colour is not easy, and some experiments will have to be made to find dust of an appropriate colour. Note that colour will change after the plastic wood has hardened and been worked.

Gluing

The best wood glues are of the PVA (or white glue) types. They are greatly superior to the old-fashioned scotch glue, and can be bought in any hardware shop.

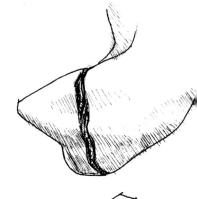

Fig. 67 Patching a split

Fig. 68 Patching a split

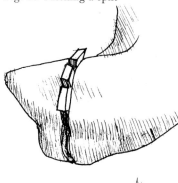

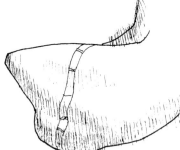

Fig. 69 *Caryatide* by Constantin Brancusi. Fogg Art Museum, Cambridge, Mass. Photo Staempfli Gallery, New York

To join two thicknesses of wood to give an adequate thickness for a proposed carving: plane the two surfaces absolutely flat. This is best done on a planing machine, or else by a professional carpenter or joiner. Coat both surfaces with glue and cramp up until set. Ensure that the grain in both pieces correspond, otherwise there is a danger that the two blocks may warp away from each other and the join open up (fig. 40C).

Finishing

On p. 55 the alternative finishes are mentioned—chiselled or smoothed. Both finishes have their attractions. A chisel finish consists of numerous small planes or planishes, which give a kind of sparkle to the work. This can be seen in much medieval church carving. The final cuts of the gouge follow and express the form. In the hands of a skilled carver, this finish is lively and crisp.

A smoothed finish expresses the quality of the wood, the pattern of the grain and the variations of colour. It is desirable where the grain is an important factor, which will enhance rather than detract from the form.

The two finishes may be used in combination.

It is usual to give wood sculpture some kind of surface treatment. A good wax polish will do, or beeswax dissolved in pure turpentine, which gives a gentle lustre. Waxing helps to bring out the quality of colour and grain, but some of the dense and oily woods will be found to require no treatment.

To prevent dirt getting into the grain, which is very difficult to remove, it is usual to seal the fibres with a resin or polyurethane clear varnish. This is applied in thin coats until it begins to show as a shine on the surface. When dry it is rubbed down with fine abrasive paper, then the wax is applied.

A high polish is obtained by applying clear varnish, rubbing down with fine abrasive paper and carefully cleaning away all dust between each application.

Sculptures for outdoors can be treated with a proprietary clear wood preservative, but some deterioration must be expected, especially on end grain and joints.

Painting is done as on the woodwork in buildings: undercoat and topcoat according to manufacturer's instructions, with priming for outdoor work.

Appendix I Typical tools and equipment for beginning

The following chisels and gouges make a reasonably balanced set for beginning carving:

No. 1 —16 mm. ($\frac{3}{4}$ in.)   No. 6*—28 mm. ($\frac{7}{8}$ in.)

No. 2 — 7 mm. ($\frac{1}{4}$ in.)   No. 7— 8 mm. ($\frac{5}{16}$ in.)

No. 3 —22 mm. ($\frac{7}{8}$ in.)   No. 8*— 7 mm. ($\frac{1}{4}$ in.)

No. 4 —11 mm. ($\frac{7}{16}$ in.)   No. 9*—19 mm. ($\frac{3}{4}$ in.)

No. 5*—13 mm. ($\frac{1}{2}$ in.)   No. 11*— 5 mm. ($\frac{3}{16}$ in.)

No. 6*—13 mm. ($\frac{1}{2}$ in.)

Those marked with an asterisk could be considered a minimum set, although if only small work is to be done, the two largest could be left out. No. 1 can be replaced with a carpenter's chisel. Add to the original set as and when the need for a particular size and shape makes itself felt. It is sometimes possible to buy second-hand gouges, but do not be tempted to take a lot of narrow ones—they are not used very often and to have more than a few is a waste of money that would be better spent on larger tools.

Carver's mallet (lignum vitae or beech), the heaviest that can be handled reasonably.

Fig. 70 Mask. Polychrome wood, Borneo
Horniman Museum, London

Fig. 71 Figure (Probably a canoe house ornament). Wood, Solomon Islands.
Horniman Museum, London

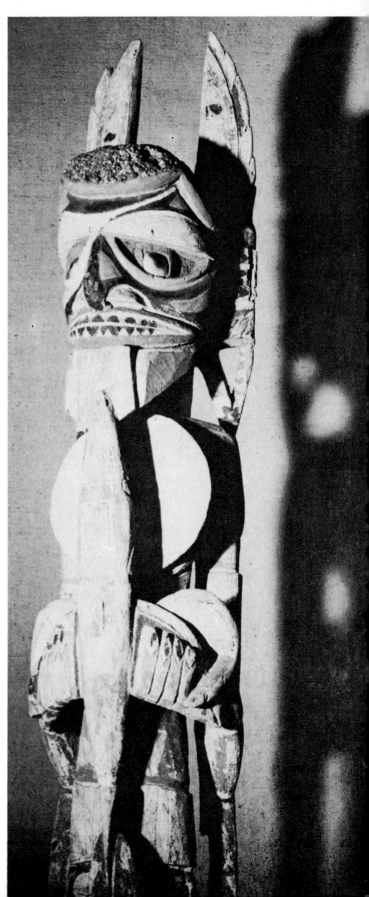

Fig. 72 Fertility figure. Wood,
Afo, Nigeria.
Horniman Museum, London

Fig. 73 Figure in memory of
the dead. Polychrome wood,
New Ireland.
Horniman Museum, London

Indiastone, medium and fine (or combination).
Slips to fit gouges.
Strop.
Abrading and carpenters' tools as required.
Bench, with firm legs and heavy top.
Vice, cramps, etc. for fixing wood.

Appendix 2

This list describes briefly the most useful softwoods and hard-woods, those foreign woods most likely to be held by stockists, and one or two of the best known exotic woods. All mentioned here carve well. See Reading list, p. 94, and List of suppliers list, p. 94 for further information.

SOFTWOODS

Cedar: there are a number of types. Red is rather brittle and soft but carves easily. Yellow is harder.

Columbia pine (douglas fir): A firm pine with attractive markings. As with most pines, it demands simple forms.

Pitch pine: the densest of the pines, with attractive markings.

Yellow pine: A light, pale pine that carves cleanly with sharp tools. Much used in the past, e.g. for ships' figureheads and even ornate picture frames.

Hemlock: a light softwood with strong markings like columbia pine.

Yew: close-grained, hard, reddish brown heartwood.

HARDWOODS

Afrormosia: firm yellowy brown wood, darkens on exposure to air. Sometimes called substitute teak.

Apple: all fruitwoods are hard. Apple is firm, reddish, close-grained.

Ash: tough, pale wood, with wide, clearly-marked grain.

Beech: very tough, hard, even wood. Tends to twist, pale pink, with small silvery flecks.

Birch: an attractive pale brown close-grained hardwood.

Cherry: hard, even, golden brown wood, good for carving.

Ebony: very hard black or dark brown, exotic wood, very expensive. Carves well.

Elm: brown, hard wood. Works well and has a broad, attractive grain.

Hickory: somewhat similar to ash but darker.

Iroko: similar to afrormosia but more golden, and less attractive, with less-varied grain.

Jarrah: dark red wood, also called Australian mahogany. Coarse, but even.

Jelutong: an unattractive yellowish wood. Very even, and cuts very cleanly. Used for pattern-making.

Lignum Vitae: a very hard, heavy wood. Sapwood, which is yellow, almost as hard as the purple-brown heartwood. Used for mallets, etc.

Lime: creamy white, soft, even, clean-cutting. Much used for delicate carving, particularly in Germany, along with pearwood, which is similarly even-grained, but hard.

Mahogany: there are a number of mahoganys which come from Central and South America, the West Indies and Africa. They all work well, being fine and clean cutting, though tending to splinter if not carved with care. They are usually pale, pinkish brown in colour, darkening and becoming yellower on exposure to the air. Honduras mahogany is often considered the best. The African mahoganys are rather soft.

Muhuhu: heavy, dense, red-brown wood, with strong, attractive grain. Tough and hard, but beautiful.

Pear: hard, even, fine-grained, pinky brown. Used for fine carving and wood engraving.

Plum: younger wood is pinkish, older wood violet brown. Sapwood, yellowish, can be used.

Rosewood: an exotic, used for furniture. Stripy black and red in colour. Even textured. Expensive.

Sapele: attractive African redwood, rather curly grain (African mahogany).

Sycamore: a kind of maple. Hard, clean, pale wood with light but distinct grain.

Teak: yellow brown with dark streaks, pink and green zones and white flecks. Blunts chisels quickly.

Utile: Another African mahogany. Darker than sapele, with firmer, more attractive grain.

Walnut: beautiful, hard, grey-brown or chocolate brown. Close grained and hard to carve.

Stone

Many people are intimidated by the thought of carving stone, but very little is required in the way of tools. A solid bench or table, a few claw tools and chisels (or, with the very soft stones, old carpenter's gouges), a hammer or mallet, and any rasps or files that may be available are all you need. A coarse oilstone or a broken piece of old paving stone does for sharpening the tools. The only other requirement is a workplace where chips of stone and some dust do not matter. In summertime there is nothing better than working out of doors.

How does the beginner choose a stone? It may be a question of what is available locally, or what can be obtained from the site of a demolished building. Soft stones are used in some areas for building or for interior work, otherwise they will have to be obtained through merchants. Chalk can be carved by young children, and blocks may be picked up under chalk cliffs. Rough lumps of alabaster are found in some parts of the country and they and blocks of soapstone can be bought (see p. 94).

The various stones cover an immense range of qualities—even more than does wood. Some are so soft they can be cut with a knife or shaped with a hacksaw blade—some are so hard that they can be worked only with specially hardened tools, slowly and patiently.

In the trade, masons and merchants often refer to 'stone', meaning sandstone and limestone only. So you may find a yard where they talk about 'stone' and 'marble'. In this book I refer to all stones as 'stone', whatever their type, because the sculptor does not usually specialize but works in whatever stone takes his fancy or is required by his client.

Try and avoid a hard stone to begin with. A soft or medium limestone is good for the beginner, but a hard, intractable stone requires patience and skill to work, and should be tackled only after some experience.

Types

There are three major classifications of rock: igneous, sedimentary and metamorphic.

Igneous rocks are the old rocks formed by cooling of the earth. They include granite, diorite and basalt.

Sedimentary rocks are formed by the breaking down of the igneous rocks, the resultant of which is deposited in layers. Limestones and sandstones were formed in this way.

Metamorphic rock is one of the former that has been changed by heat and/or pressure to a new form. Marble, which comes from limestone, is an example.

More important than these classifications to the sculptor are the qualities of the main carving stones.

LIMESTONES

These include some of the softest stones. Chalk can loosely be classified in this group. Some of the true limestones are almost as soft. At the other end of the scale are the so-called English marbles, such as Purbeck marble and Hopton Wood, which are so hard that they take as good a polish as true marble. Many of the limestones contain shells, some being composed almost entirely of shell, cemented together in a solid mass. These stones are usually hard to work. Some limestones, on the other hand, are almost or completely shell-free.

The oolitic limestones consist of a mass of tiny, spherical granules cemented together by carbonate of lime. They may be very fine, or they may be quite coarse and easily discernible. These stones often contain shell, which is harder than the surrounding stone. When a shell is found to be in the way, work round it so that it stands proud and then either chip it or hacksaw it off. Oolitic limestones are used a lot for building and are popular with sculptors. Those known as Bath stones are usually soft, coarse grained and easily worked. But it is dangerous to generalize about stone, and sometimes Bath stone can be very hard.

Carboniferous limestones do not have the 'fish roe' texture of the oolitic limestones, but vary from soft to hard in quality.

Magnesian limestones are similar in quality to the carboniferous.

SANDSTONES

Many people are under the misapprehension that sandstone is soft and easily worked. Some sandstones are, but many are hard and intractable. All of them blunt chisels much more quickly than do the limestones. The fact that the 'gritstone' variety of sandstone is used for both paving stones and for grindstones demonstrated the toughness and abrasive quality that can be found.

A number of these stones are used by sculptors. Colours vary from red and brown to cream and near white, and blue-grey. Texture is from very fine to very coarse.

Some of the sandstones contain a lot of silica, so the dust may be harmful or even dangerous. When working siliceous stones they should either be kept damp (this also assists the carving quality in some cases) or a dust mask should be worn. Many masons do not do this, and will swear that no harm comes to them; but silica damages the lungs and precautions should be taken.

All stones, but sandstone in particular, is more easily carved when newly quarried. Freestone is a term used to describe sandstones which are even in texture, with no marked bed (i.e. layers), and which can be worked readily into blocks. The term is also applied to limestones.

If a sculpture in sedimentary stone is to be placed out of doors, it should be carved so that the bed is horizontal. If placed vertically, penetration of wet is likely to be greater and deterioration quicker. This is particularly true of some of the sandstones but also applies to the limestones.

MARBLE

This is a metamorphic limestone. At some stage most carvers will want to try it, for it has a glamour and beauty of its own. It ranges in colour from white to black, and is also streaked in a variety of colours. There is no bed, and the crystalline quality of the material takes a high polish. Tools have to be harder than for the sedimentary stones, and it is chipped away in smallish pieces rather than cut.

GRANITE

This hard, intractable stone is widely distributed. It has great beauty of colour and takes a fine polish. Unless you live in a predominantly granite area, gain experience on easier stones before tackling it.

ALABASTER

This is a well-compacted, fine-grained form of gypsum (from which plaster of paris is made). It is often transluscent, white or cream in colour, but sometimes opaque brown, and sometimes a mixture of these. Soft, easily worked, but fragile, it takes a fine polish.

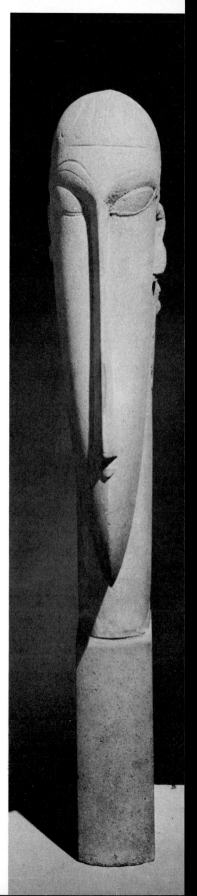

Fig. 74 *Head* by Amadeo Modigliani.
Tate Gallery, London

SLATE

A metamorphic stone, can be split in narrow sheets, when it is used for roofing. Some kinds are suitable for relief carving and for lettering. The colour can vary from purple to green. It is not often obtainable in blocks suitable for working in the round.

SOAPSTONE

A soft stone, usually light to dark grey, a hard form of talc. It has a characteristically greasy feel. Steatite, a variety of talc, varies from white-grey, yellow to green and has the appearance of marble. These stones work easily with simple tools.

Tools

The carver uses chisel-like tools made from an octagonal steel bar which is shaped on an anvil by a tool-smith and made hard by tempering.

Pitcher—a broad, blunt-ended tool used for clearing large volumes of stone.

Point, punch—a heavy tool with a point or nearly pointed end, used for rough working. (Marble point is pointed, limestone or sandstone punch slightly broad.)

Claw—a chisel with a toothed edge (pointed teeth for marble, flat teeth for freestones) for major development work. The teeth are filed in after smithing but before tempering.

Fig. 75 Pestle, in the form of a bird. Stone, age uncertain, from Papua, New Guinea.
British Museum, London

Fig. 76 Mask. Stone, Aztec, probably fourteenth century.
British Museum, London

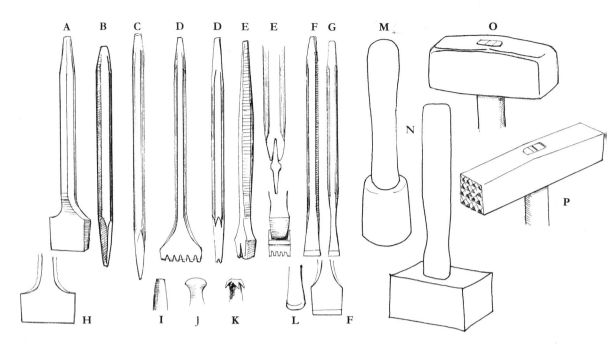

A B C D D E E F G M O N P H I J K L F

Fig. 78 Using pitcher

Fig. 79 Using pitcher

Fig. 77 Stone-carving tools.
A pitcher
B punch
C point
D claw
E claw bit and holder
F chisel
G lettering chisel
H bolster
I hammer head
J mallet head
K burred head caused by hammering, should be filed off
L bullnose chisel
M dummy
N iron lump hammer
O steel hammer
P bouchard or bush hammer

Chisel—describes itself, a straight-edged tool for finishing surfaces. May be obtained with inset (tungsten) tip for working gritstones and highly abrasive stones.

Gouge—like chisel, but curved.

Bullnose chisel or claw—a chisel or claw with the end rounded.

Bolster—a wide chisel used for working large flat surfaces.

Hammer head—a tool (point, claw, etc.) with a small head intended for use with a hammer.

Mallet head—a tool with a mushroom head intended for use with a mallet. Should not be used with a hammer.

Hammer—generally speaking the best sort of hammer is made of soft iron. Like the dummy, and unlike a steel hammer (which tends to bounce off the chisel head), it gives a dull blow. Weight 1 lb–4 lb.

Mallet—a wood mallet usually made of beech is used, particularly by masons, for working the softer stones. A mallet large enough for heavy work would be inconvenient and inefficient, but the soft, stunning blow it gives makes it suitable for masonry work. There is an area where it is a question of choice between a mallet and a light hammer or dummy.

Dummy—a small mallet made of metal alloy, used for light work and finishing. Gives a dull blow and does not bounce off the chisel-head.

Rasp—a coarse, file-like tool used for working limestones and marble, but not sandstones and granite.

Riffler—shaped rasps for working difficult corners, hollows, etc. Bought in varying shapes and sizes (see woodcarving p. 44).

Bouchard—a hammer with the face cut as teeth, used for bruising off the surface of the stone. Care must be taken that the bruising does not go deeper than intended. Its misuse can lead to flabby, unrealized forms (see p. 77).

Drag—a flat piece of metal with a straight, toothed edge, used for working off surfaces on soft stones.

Cocks-comb—a flat piece of metal, edges cut to various shapes and toothed. Used as is the drag, but for mouldings and odd-shaped hollows.

Carborundum—an artificial stone used for smoothing.

Snakestone—a fine natural stone used for polishing, particularly marble; especially in difficult corners.

Power tools—these are used as point, claw or chisel bits in a pneumatic or reciprocating drill. Used today in commercial yards and by sculptors who work a lot in stone. The drill must be of an industrial capacity, otherwise no benefit is obtained.

Care and maintenance of tools

SHARPENING

Sculptors and masons always keep a piece of gritstone available to sharpen chisels, etc., which has to be done pretty constantly. Water is used as a lubricant. A piece of carborundum can be used instead, and this is essential if using tungsten-tipped chisels.

It is usual to use a number of chisels or claws rather than one. They are used until blunt, and then all sharpened at once.

When cutting letters or doing very fine work, a fine sharpening stone, such as a washita or an arkansas can be used to put a really fine edge on the chisel (see p. 47).

DRAWING OUT OR REMAKING

After continuous resharpening the taper on a chisel is unduly worn and the blade becomes too thick. With a claw the teeth become too short and thick. Points also become too broad. Then the tool has to be taken to the toolsmith to be softened in the forge, rehammered on the anvil and retempered. By this means tools can be used for a very long time, if not indefinitely, before they become too short for convenience.

Tempering consists of heating the tool in a fire until the end is at the appropriate temperature (indicated by the colour) and then plunging it in a can of suitable oil (e.g. linseed oil) so that it cools suddenly.

The principle is that the harder the stone to be worked, the harder the steel. But the harder the steel, the more brittle and likely to break, so the tool is kept as soft as is consonant with the work it has to do. Although this is a highly skilled craft, tempering is sometimes done by the sculptor himself. Heat the working end of the chisel to cherry red (not to white heat, when the metal may be spoilt) and drop in the oil. The chisel is now very hard. Emery cloth it clean. Play a blow or propane torch flame on it about one inch from the end. The colours will move along to the tip as it heats up, and when the appropriate colour reaches the end, drop the chisel in the oil to cool it. The colours are straw for marble, bronze for hard limestones, blue for soft limestones. The colours appear in the order indicated.

Equipment

The sculptor in stone needs very little equipment, unless he is working with large pieces of stone. Even then, with careful manoeuvring, large pieces of stone can be manipulated with very little equipment.

Banker—solidly built work bench. Square is probably the most

Fig. 80 Sharpening a chisel
A shoulder too high: when the chisel becomes too thick to sharpen properly, it must be returned to the toolsmith for reforging
B shoulder correct

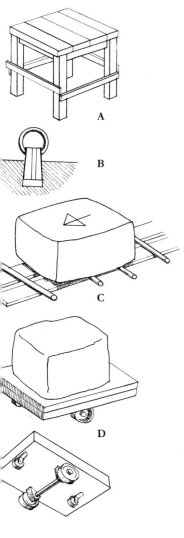

useful shape for the sculptor. Height will depend on work being carried out, but for small work approximately 825 mm. (33 ins) is convenient. A heavy table, reinforced if necessary, can suffice.

Spirit level.

Straight edge (steel).

Try square (carpenter's square).

Crow bar, lever, blocks, etc. if required.

Moving stone

Obviously stone is heavy for its bulk (on the average say 2000–2500 kilos per cubic metre, 120–140 lbs per cubic foot). Where block and tackle is available, a lewis (fig. 81B) is used for lifting large blocks. Where a lewis hole cannot be made, slings should be used.

A large block is moved by means of rollers where hoist and tackle is not available. Two or three lengths of steel pipe are used, each pipe being carried to the front as it drops free at the back. A method that is used to turn stone is to lever one side up, place a pebble or strip of wood (known as a miller) in the centre, thus enabling it to be turned quite easily.

A sampson is used for moving stone about. It is a low trolley with two iron wheels in the middle and a smaller one at either end. This enables uneven surfaces to be negotiated. On the studio floor a trolley with four iron wheels can be used; in fig. 87 such a trolley is used as a banker.

Stone may be raised by levering up and blocking first one side, then the other, alternating until the required height is reached. You are dealing with a heavy and potentially dangerous weight, so ensure that the blocking is substantial and secure.

Pad edges when levering with a piece of wood. Pressure on the edge of a piece of stone will cause it to flake and chip. Also pad edges with wood and/or sacking when turning a block. The weight of a block will crumble a fine edge.

Do not try to save a falling block—get out of the way. Quarrymen and others working with large blocks use boots with steel toecaps. While the sculptor would not in the ordinary way need to do this, the warning is there—keep toes away from blocks of stone, and the same goes for fingers. Small pieces of wood placed under the block will allow space and prevent crushed fingers.

Holding methods

Large blocks of stone hold themselves in position, the problem being to turn them if necessary (see above).

Fig. 81

A banker

B lewis—one of various types: two wedge-shaped pieces of steel are dropped into a tapered hole in the stone, and a third leaf placed between them to hold them apart; all are suspended on a ring which is used for lifting

C moving stone by means of rollers

D sampson

Small blocks may have their bases cut in a rectangular form so that a box of strong battens, screwed to the bench or banker, can be built round them.

For a sculpture that is to be completely in the round, pads of old sacks, foamed rubber or foamed plastic are good, strong canvas bags filled with sand are also used.

Relief panels or panels of lettering may be supported on a kind of easel. If much of this work is done, it is worth having a frame attached to the wall with two adjustable horizontal members bolted to the verticals. It is usual to plaster a thin panel of stone onto a heavier block of stone for relief or letter carving. Soak both block and panel well, make a fairly stiff plaster mix, spread on the block and press the panel onto it, holding in position until the plaster goes off (plaster mix p. 82).

The panel can be levered off when the work is completed.

Working stone

As with all materials, a block of stone should only be used in a manner appropriate to its nature. One thing all stones have in common is that unlike wood, long slender elements are invariably fragile. Almost all ancient figures have been broken at the legs, and many have their arms broken too. Some craftsmen have always taken pride in pushing a material as far as it will go, but in general this is not good practice and the nature of the material should always be born in mind when designing.

All stones have innate characteristics which impose their requirements on the sculptor, and he ignores them at his peril.

The softer and coarser stones, such as many of the Bath stones, have to be treated simply and in rather block-like terms; whereas hard, close-grained stones such as marble or soft, close-grained ones such as alabaster can be worked very delicately. Hard, intractable stones such as granite are treated simply, because of the difficulty inherent in working them. Other stones will be found more or less hard, and more or less close-grained, the inherent qualities making their demands on the treatment.

Resistance to weather and atmospheric pollution is another important factor. Most marbles resist weather quite well. Many of the limestones and sandstones need introducing to inclement weather gradually (i.e. fixing in position during the summer) to allow the surface to develop a tough crust (case-hardening). Some are not suitable for exterior use, the soft limestones and alabaster, for example.

If a sculpture is to be placed in the open air it, should be carved so that the bed (layers of stone) is horizontal. If the bed is vertical, freezing water is more likely to get inside it and break pieces off.

Cutting a block

There are a number of ways of cutting a block from a larger piece. Nowadays stone is usually cut by machine in a masons's yard. By this means a block with square sides or whatever is desired can be obtained easily. But if the block is obtained from a demolition site, then its shape may be quite inappropriate and, while it may be possible to have it cut professionally in a yard, it may be necessary for the carver to cut it up himself:

1 Mark the block that is to be cut off.
2 With a point or punch make a deep groove all round, along the line. If too heavy to turn, groove on the three exposed sides.
3 Wedge up the main block and place a steel bar under the proposed line of cleavage so that the block to be cut off is suspended slightly above the ground.
4 Work round the groove with a bolster until the block falls off.

Figs 82–83 Unfinished carvings, Portland stone. Note simplicity of shape appropriate to the material, and degree of development achieved with the various tools

Fig. 82

Fig. 83

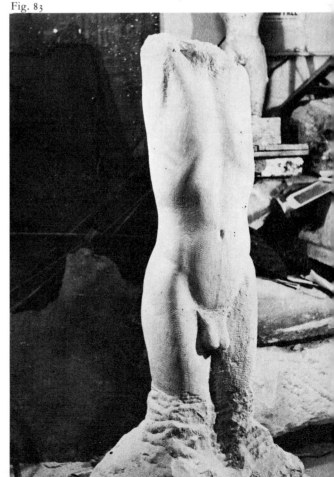

Similar to above: make a series of narrow holes round the proposed line of cleavage, and equally spaced at, say seventy to one hundred millimetre intervals. Into these insert small steel wedges, and by careful, systematic tapping the block should break on the desired line.

Note that cutting a block in this way is not very dependable. The block should be examined carefully to ensure that, so far as can be ascertained, there is no fault line along which it will split in preference to the desired one, and care should be taken to tap evenly round the line.

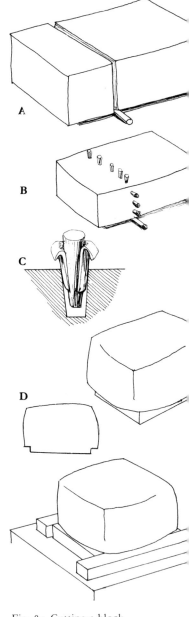

Fig. 84 Cutting a block
A with groove
B with wedges
C wedge and feather (increases efficiency of wedge and prevents it enlarging the sides of the hole)
D Holding a block, base squared-up and held with battens (wood strips)

LEVELLING A SURFACE

1 Determine the proposed line at one end of the block and cut a small area level at either end with point and claw.
2 Place two small blocks of wood of equal thickness on these level areas and lay a straight-edge across. A straight piece of wood will do.
3 Repeat 1 and 2 at the other end, lining up the undersides of the two straight-edges by eye.
4 Join the four level corners, by working off the stone between them and checking with a straight-edge.
5 Work lines across, checking with the straight-edge.
6 Work off remainder of surplus stone.

To level another surface at right-angles to the first, do the same, checking the right-angle with a square or with spirit level and plumb-line, or with a pre-cut template (usually made in sheet metal).

BOASTING

With a large figure it is sometimes possible to give the mason a 'boasting' drawing, which shows large volumes that may be cut away (fig. 16A). If this is done with care, the stone which has been removed can be in the form of very useful blocks. The use or resale of these may make a very considerable saving in the price of a job. Allow enough for base and/or fixing while carving.

ROUGHING-OUT

This is done with coarse tools, usually the pitcher and point. With a very soft stone it may be done with pitcher and large claw only.

It consists of taking off major volumes and, especially, getting rid of the squareness of the block. Generally speaking one works from high point to high point. Pitcher and point are held at a steep angle to the stone to stun pieces off (figs 78, 87).

DEVELOPING

Forms are developed with fine point and claw, moving towards the final form but not committing oneself by undercutting until sure that the cut is in the right place.

The claw is held at a shallower angle than the heavy point. Note that while the height is probably fixed by the height of the stone, it is the width that has to decrease, so the figure looks lumpy and ill-proportioned. Do not be tempted to adjust this. Mark major levels on the stone and stick to them.

Keep an approximately even level of development over the whole sculpture. One part should not be much more finished than the rest, although for the sake of strength it may be necessary to keep the lower part thick until the upper is quite far advanced. Any slender part may need to be either left thick or buttressed with a column of stone until quite a late stage. This is necessary because the vibration set up by continuous blows may cause a slender part to crack through.

Shells in limestones should be worked round and either chipped off or sawn through and finished with file or riffler.

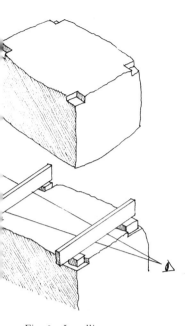

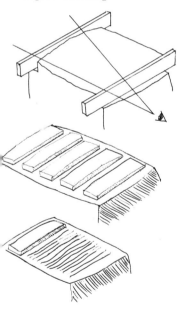

Fig. 85 Levelling
Fig. 86 Levelling

Fig. 87 Carving Portland stone, trolley used as banker

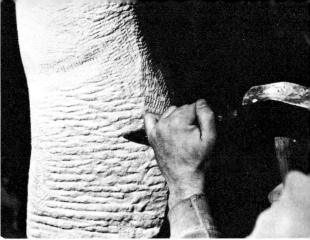

Fig. 88 Carving Portland stone,
roughing-out with heavy punch

Fig. 89 Carving Portland stone,
roughing-out with heavy punch

Fig. 90 Carving Portland stone,
roughing-out with fine point

Fig. 91 Carving marble,
developing with point

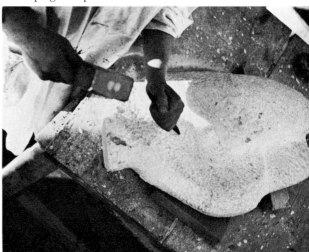

Fig. 92 Carving marble,
developing with claw

Fig. 93 Carving Portland stone,
developing with claw

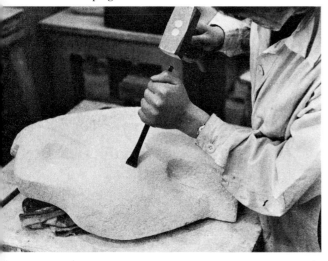

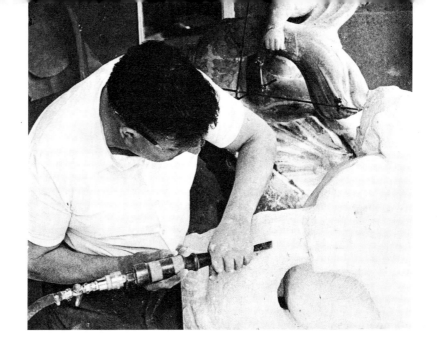

Fig. 94 Carving limestone, developing with power tool (chisel, driven by compressed air)

The developing is continued with fine claws almost to the finished stage. The whole procedure has something of the quality of an unveiling process. Once the figure is roughed out it can be seen, wrapped under layers of stone. These layers are steadily peeled away with point and claw. Deep hollows and incisions remain covered with the layers of stone, but as these layers are removed, the forms appear more clearly. Finally the finished sculpture is there, but covered, as though with a fine muslin.

Finishing

The method described above may be considered a classical approach, with the final result to be either chiselled or polished.

Not only may other tools and methods be used, as described on p. 77, but, clearly, there is no one way of finishing. A sculpture may be finished entirely with the point, or it may be highly polished.

The point leaves as coarse a finish as the sculptor wishes. It will be found that parallel lines of point marks tend to arise during the developing process (fig. 87). These give a particular quality in the way they reflect the light, and are very different from the random point marks of initial massing out.

The claw also leaves a textured surface but very much finer, and, if using a worn claw, the surface is almost smooth.

Finishing with a chisel is the last in the scale of tooled finishes.

Claw and chisel must be sharp, with not too heavy a shoulder on the cutting edge. This is so that the angle at which the tool is held to the stone is shallow. If it is not shallow, and if the tool is not sharp,

75

there is a danger of plucking (small pieces of stone coming away, and leaving the surface pitted).

Hollows are worked either with a gouge (in soft stones) or, more usually, with a bullnosed claw or chisel. This has a rounded end and consequently forms a hollow.

The chisel leaves a smooth finish, which tends to be slightly faceted. Designing for a chisel finish should take account of this. The kind of finish to be expected can be seen in much Gothic and Romanesque carving.

ABRASIVES

A smoother, unfaceted finish is obtained by smoothing with abrasives. Which one is used will depend on the stone being smoothed and the degree of finish required. File and riffler are the initial abrasives.

Almost anything will wear away the soft Bath stones. Limestones in general, and all other stones, can be abraded with a piece of grit-stone or carborundum blocks of varying grades. Pumice stone is an intermediate abrasive for fine stones.

Garnet paper, wet-or-dry paper and emery cloth may be used on fine stones. Fine wet-or-dry used wet is a good final abrasive.

Polishing

Many stones will not take a polish. This includes all the coarser oolitic limestones and the sandstones. Some limestones, such as Portland, take quite a good polish and the hard ones such as Purbeck marble take a polish equal to marble. Granite, alabaster and, indeed, all the close-grained stones can be polished. With these stones, particularly the figured ones, their true beauty only comes out with polishing. It is done by smoothing with finer and finer abrasives, until the stone is free of scratches. The amount of labour involved will depend on the hardness of the stone. Alabaster can be polished quite easily, but the hard ones are much more laborious.

Once the surface is as smooth as possible and all scratches are removed, the stone is ready for its final polish. Work the whole surface with snakestone or, if not available, with pumice powder. Finish with putty powder. The fine dust of the stone itself can also be used. Use water as a lubricant. When as polished as possible, a thin coat of wax or a touch of thin oil, polished with a soft cloth, will give the final lustre.

It must be appreciated that a high polish demands both a simple and a perfect form. Irregularities and unresolved forms will become more obvious than when left with a chiselled or rough finish.

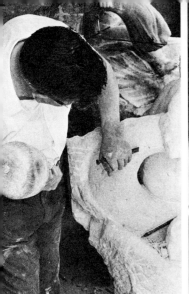

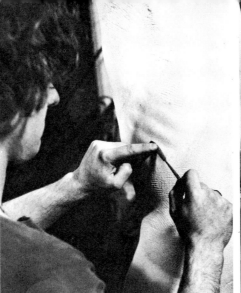

Fig. 95 Carving limestone, finishing with mallet-head chisel and mallet

Fig. 96 Carving Portland stone, using riffler

Fig. 97 Carving marble, using wet-or-dry carborundum paper (see also figs 19–25 on alabaster carving)

Additional means of working stone

Cock-combs are sometimes used on the soft limestones, particularly for shaping-up mouldings, but also on sculptures for working awkward corners. They consist of shaped pieces of sheet-metal with teeth (hence the name) and are dragged along the stone, crumbling it away. They can have teeth of varying sizes.

Drags, with a straight, concave or convex-toothed edge, are used for removing toolmarks from plain surfaces on the soft stones.
Rasps work in a somewhat similar way but, as with filing wood and metal, a considerable amount of shaping and developing can be done. Here lies the main danger of the tool, in that there is a temptation to use it at too early a stage so that the sculpture remains overblown and bulbous and the forms are insensitive. Point and claw are the main tools for most of the work, but the rasp is a valuable ancilliary. Rifflers have been described under woodcarving (p. 44). They consist of shaped rasps or files which can be used for developing awkward forms and working difficult or inaccessible corners.
The bouchard or bush hammer is used, particularly, on the hard stones, to crumble away areas. Its dangers are similar to those described for the rasp, but there is a further danger to consider when using it with crystalline stones such as marble; this is that the stone may be bruised much more deeply than intended. Consequently the tool must be used judiciously both from the technical point of view and also the aesthetic.

Fig. 98 *Tondo* by Michelangelo. Note varying stages worked with heavy point, light point, claw, chisel, and finish with abrasives. The figure on the left is approaching the stage where the final skin of stone will be taken off with the chisel.
Royal Academy of Arts, London

Woodcarving gouges can be used on the very soft stones such as Beer (see Appendix 2 p. 79), alabaster, chalk, soapstone.

Surform and various improvized tools may also be used on these stones.

Power tools are widely used both by masons and by sculptors carrying out large works. A source of power is needed, such as an industrial drill with a vibratory action. A flexible drive attachment is best, and to this is fixed a bit consisting of a point, a claw or a chisel. A lot of the heavy labour attached to working the harder stones is avoided by this means. Some sculptors still prefer to use hand tools, however, and I know of one mason's yard where, although power is available, none of the masons use it, preferring the old, traditional methods.

Appendix I

It is not possible to give a definitive list of basic tools, as they depend on the stone being worked.

Soft stones—can be worked with old carpenter's gouges, rasp, file, rifflers; or mallet-headed stone tools: claws, chisels.

Medium stones—light punch, heavy punch, three or four varied claw tools or two claw bit holders and bits, six varied chisels. If

Fig. 99 *Hybrid fruit called Pagoda* by Jean Arp, 1934. Tate Gallery, London. Photo Etienne Bertrand Weill

working sandstone, double or treble numbers *or* use tungsten-tipped tools.

Hard stones—will require harder tempered tools.

Bench or banker of appropriate height for comfortable work, thick top.

Sharpening stone—gritstone, indiastone, or, for tungsten-tipped tools, carborundum block.

Appendix 2

SOFT STONES

Alabaster—smooth, easy to carve, but fragile. Takes a good polish. Varies from a transluscent white or pale yellow to opaque brown.

Soapstone—grey, grainy-looking colour, but smooth and fine. Will polish.

Steatite—a green version of soapstone, popular in USA.

Chalk—can be obtained in lumps—easily carved, but not very attractive.

Beer—a fine, smooth, soft limestone, nearly white. Takes fine detail —mainly interior use.

Caen—a French limestone, cream coloured, finer even than Beer.

Bathstone—There are a number of oolitic limestones in this group. They tend to be coarse in texture, easily worked, but not taking fine detail, and varying in colour from cream to yellow or pale brown. Some beds are relatively hard, however, and would be classed as medium.

African Wonderstone—a grey, sedimentary stone imported from Africa. Smooth, even consistency, carves well. Used in USA.

MEDIUM STONES

(Many of the limestones, both oolitic and others, come in this group, and also some sandstones.)

Portland—widely used cream oolitic limestone that weathers white. Can be very shelly, but basebed, which is softer, is often shell-free.

Ancaster—a creamy yellow limestone, usually softer than Portland, and even.

Clipsham—not dissimilar to Ancaster, but darker and less even, both in colour and in quality, and harder.

Indiana—an American limestone, considered to be one of the best. It is medium hard, fine, cuts well, buff to grey in colour.

Ham Hill—a coarse, yellow-brown medium sandstone. All sandstones blunt tools quickly, but this does not mean necessarily that they are hard. Tungsten-tipped chisels blunt much more slowly.

Mansfield—red or orange, even, as with most sandstones it cuts readily when 'green' (newly quarried) and toughens up as it matures.

Hollington—fine, white, even. Hardens with weathering.

Ohio—the most widely used American sandstone, varying in colour. Fine to medium.

HARD STONES

Many of the sandstones are very hard. Woodkirk is one of the most even and clean-cutting. Brown Woodkirk is dependable, blunts tools quickly. There are many others.

Marbles

Carrara—the most used Italian marble, pure white, hard, even. Often considered the best carving marble.

Sicilian—bluey-white, hard, coarser, colder.

Belgian—black or veined, hard, even, much used.

Vermont—white and a variety of colours. Highly regarded in USA.

Granites—there are numerous granites, black, grey, red, all hard and intractable.

This list is far from exhaustive, but gives a brief outline of a few of the stones available. See Reading list (p. 95) for more detailed information.

Plaster

Plaster of paris is an easy material to carve. Its main disadvantage is that it is messy. Bits that fall on the floor tend to get tramped around, so that trails of white footmarks lead away from the place of work to other places visited by the sculptor. If done in a workshop this probably does not matter, and a change of shoes at the door will obviate mess. If done on the dining room table, care, plus large dust sheets, are necessary.

Plaster is quite strong when dry, but brittle. Generally speaking it is not suitable for long slender elements, unless firmly attached to the block at either end. Quite fine work can be carried out in dry plaster if care and patience are used and the tools are sharp. When quite dry it tends to chip and flake easily, and if it is still very wet it is difficult to keep edges crisp. Pieces will break and split off very easily and sharp edges will rub. The best condition for carving is when the plaster has largely but not completely dried out, but fine abrading and smoothing is best done when it is dry.

Making a block

Fine or superfine casting plaster should be used. Do not use one of the very hard grades, such as Herculite, which is very difficult to work when set, nor a building plaster, which takes too long to go off and does not achieve its maximum strength very quickly.

A cardboard box, such as a shoe box, makes a good mould but the sides will need supporting with bricks, wood or clay, otherwise the weight of plaster will probably distort the card. Cardboard tubes are useful for smaller, cylindrical blocks. Polyethylene bowls, sandwich boxes, etc. are excellent. Plaster does not stick to polyethelene and, as it is flexible, the block can be pushed out quite easily.

Wood may be used, but the sides will either have to be nailed or supported and joints sealed.

METHOD FOR MAKING A RECTANGULAR BLOCK
1 Take a cardboard box of the appropriate size, and support the sides with firm weights such as bricks. Ensure the box will not leak.

2 Make up a mix of plaster (see below), preferably enough to fill the box at one go, and pour it into the cardboard box. Slightly overfill, so that the plaster stands above the edges of the box. When it is nearly set, strike off the surplus with a straight-edge or straight piece of wood. When set, peel off the cardboard.

Or build up a frame with pieces of board. Support with bricks and/or nail lightly. Place on a flat surface and block cracks in the joints with clay or plaster. Thinly wax inside surfaces with eg. floor wax.

3 The weight of the plaster will tend to force itself under the wood frame, and it will leak away. Therefore the frame must either be weighted heavily to counteract the weight of the plaster; or make a very small mix and pour to cover the bottom of the frame to a depth of 10 mm. to 20 mm.

Make a mix enough to fill the rest of the frame, roughen the surface of the first layer of plaster and pour the new lot in when the first batch has firmed up but is not hard. When set, dismantle the frame.

Note: If the mix is insufficient to fill the box, make a fresh batch as quickly as possible and pour. If the old batch has started to firm up, scratch the surface to aid adhesion.

When filling a cardboard tube or anything open-ended, remember that the weight of plaster will tend to force itself under the container. Ensure that the bottom is well sealed.

A PLASTER MIX
(For details of manipulation of plaster see *Starting with Sculpture* by the author)

A good mix consists of approximately equal volumes of water and plaster.

1 Pour an appropriate quantity of water into a bowl (a polyethylene basin is good for this).

2 Sprinkle into it as fast as possible an equal quantity of good dry plaster. Sprinkling it by hand enables any lumps to be extracted during the process. This must be done fast. When you have added the correct amount of plaster to the water, it will appear above the surface in places.

3 Allow the plaster to take up water for a minute or two, and then agitate the mix with the hand or a spoon *under* the surface, so as to cause as little splashing as possible; otherwise the mix will take up air bubbles and the block will not be solid.

4 When the plaster is evenly distributed throughout the water, pour it into the mould.

Fig. 100 Carving plaster, working with gouge

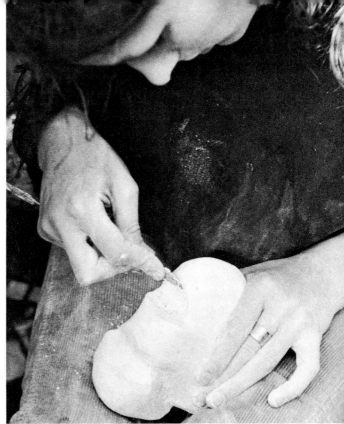

Fig. 101 Carving plaster, working with riffler

Tools

Chisels or gouges and mallet.
Knife.
Spatulas, etc.
Plaster rasps, files, rifflers, Surform.
Sandpaper.
While plaster is still soft it can be carved with almost anything metal (eg. a spoon). When dry, stronger tools are needed.

Working

A wide range of plaster tools, including spatulas, chisels, gouges and toothed spatulas can be obtained (see List of suppliers, p. 94), but generally speaking they are not necessary for carving.

Woodcarving tools can be used. It is best to use old ones, because plaster tends to blunt chisels, and if damp will cause rust unless great care is taken.

If the carving is intended as a maquette for wood, the use of wood-carving gouges and chisels will help the sculptor to realize wood-like

Fig. 102 Carving plaster, using broken Surform blade

Fig. 103 Finished maquette

forms. The texture of plaster is nothing like wood however, and direction of wood-grain must be born in mind while carving the plaster block.

The analogy between plaster and stone is much greater, so that forms which are feasible in plaster will probably be correct for stone. Difference in scale is the chief consideration. Woodcarving tools are probably better than stonecarving tools for carving plaster.

Abrading damp plaster is done with a plaster rasp, which has holes like a vegetable grater. This prevents the tools getting clogged. Broken pieces of Surform blade, especially the curved type, are useful. Dry plaster can be worked with rasps, files and rifflers. Wet plaster clogs this kind of tool.

Smoothing is done with sandpaper, starting with coarse or medium and finishing with fine. It should be done when the plaster is dry.

Usually, a plaster carving will be done for its own sake and not as a maquette. Anything useful can be brought into use. A knife can be made from a broken hacksaw blade, ground down and partly bound with string for a handle. Old kitchen knives, saw blades, files, etc. can all be used. Holes can be drilled with a flat piece of metal such as a hacksaw blade or (for small holes) a piece of soft wire hammered flat and filed square, twisted backwards and forwards. Plaster can also be sawn, preferably with a saw with teeth set wide, so that a substantial groove is cut which will not bind on the sides of the saw.

Intaglio

A special form of plaster carving is the cutting of a relief in reverse, so that a cast taken from it becomes a positive. This was done in reverse in stone in Ancient Babylonia, where little cylinders cut in this form were used as seals, much as signet rings are used on sealing wax.

METHOD
1 Cast a suitably-sized block of plaster. Let it dry.
2 Mark on it the proposed design.
3 Cut away with small tools. Old dentist's tools are ideal for fine work. Tools can be made from soft wire, hammered flat and filed to shape.
4 To see how the work is going, press in a piece of plasticine or soft clay and examine the imprint. Remember that the deepest cut will be highest in the relief. Although at first it is difficult to think in reverse, with a little practice it becomes quite easy.

The positive of this intaglio may be made in clay, by pressing when soft, drying and firing. If to be made in plaster, the relief should be sealed with several thin coats of shellac, lightly oiled or waxed and the plaster poured onto this.

Casts can also be made in lead. Ensure that the carving is completely dry (a damp mould will cause the lead to explode), rub graphite over it and pour the molten lead.

Note: Ensure that there are no undercuts on the intaglio relief, otherwise the cast will not come away from it cleanly.

Aeriated concrete building blocks

Fig. 104 Wall, thermalite block, by students of Central London Polytechnic

This material is used widely in the building industry for internal walls. It is made of pulverized ash and sand, bound with cement, and aeriated to achieve lightness.

There are a number of similar blocks marketed under various trade names, which may be obtained in a variety of sizes, usually 450 mm. long, 150–300 mm. wide, and from 50 mm. to approximately 300 mm. thick. Trade names in USA are Pumice Block, Waylite, Colite, Leelite.

They are usually a dull grey in colour, of smooth, spongey texture, often fine, but sometimes rather coarse. This variation will depend on the particular brand and grade and, while it may have little effect for building purposes, it does affect the quality for carving. Normal finish is a roughish, zig-zag marked surface; but smooth and textured fair-face finish may also be had.

There are other kinds of building blocks made of coarser, denser concrete, which are not suitable for carving. They are known as lightweight or heavyweight building blocks. Their hardness, coarseness and weight readily identify them.

Advantages and disadvantages: the chief advantage of this material is its ready availability, cheapness, and the ease with which it can be carved. Odd pieces can often be obtained from building sites. Quite quick results can be achieved, which makes it suitable for children to work with. It is also capable of more sophisticated treatment.

Its main disadvantage is its unpleasant dustiness. It is better to use it out of doors, as the air tends to become filled with a fine, irritating dust which descends as a fine deposit over everything. The material can be wetted to keep dust down, but this makes it even more fragile than it already it. As the dust is unpleasant and irritating, a dust mask is advantageous.

Tools and equipment

Building block may be worked very readily. It can be sawn, carved and scored. Old woodcarving, carpentry and stonecarving chisels, claws and gouges can be used. Although it is so easy to work, it blunts tools very quickly and chisels will require frequent resharpening. Sharpen on an oilstone or on a piece of gritstone (see stonecarving p. 68 and woodcarving p. 45). Rasps, files, rifflers, Surform, old hacksaw blades can also be used. Coarse emery cloth or sandpaper may be used for smoothing.

A bench, banker or strong table of suitable height, with a thick pad of sacking or sandbag should be used. Edges chip easily, and vibration from blows with hammer and chisel will crack the block unless padding is adequate.

Electric tools can be used. An orbital sander with aluminium oxide disc or similar may be useful, but will cause a lot of dust. Shot-blasting has also been used. This requires sophisticated equipment and protective clothing, which is available in the building industry (fig. 105).

Working

The nature of the material is such that designs must be broad in treatment. No great degree of delicacy is possible, and fine work will tend to crumble.

When working with hammer or mallet and chisel, it is particularly important not to lever or pry off pieces. Always ensure that the piece being cut away is weaker than the piece remaining. Any undue levering will cause the block to break. Holes may be drilled quite easily, even with a flat piece of metal such as a hacksaw blade, twisted with a rotary movement.

Major shapes can also be sawn out. Saws with a number of narrow, detachable blades of varying types can be bought cheaply and are excellent for this purpose.

Once major forms are developed, abrading tools are the most satisfactory, as there is less chance of pieces being broken off.

Finishing

The usual method is to finish with abrasives, files, etc. or abrasive paper, and to leave the material in its natural colour. It can also be painted. Alkali-resisting paint should be used; plastic-emulsion is suitable. Thoroughly clean off all dust before painting. The finish will not be absolutely smooth because of the porous character of the material.

opposite
Fig. 106 Carving by pupil of Reydon Modern School, Southwold, Suffolk. Concrete block

Fig. 107. Carving by pupil of Reydon Modern School, Southwold, Suffolk. Concrete block

Fig. 105 *Architecture through the ages* by William Mitchell. Shot-blasted from thermalite blocks. Photo Crispin Eurich. Courtesy Thermalite Ltd

Brick

This material is not widely used, although some major sculptures have been carried out in it. Notable is Henry Moore's large relief on the Bon Centrum building in Rotterdam. Worthy of note too are the carvings by Eric Kennington on the Shakespeare Memorial Theatre, Stratford on Avon.

As is true with most of the materials suitable for carving, brick can be treated in two ways: a single brick can be carved with minimum tools and almost no equipment, or the whole process can be treated on a much more sophisticated level as a major sculptural work.

Bricks are of two kinds: clay and sand-lime. The latter, which are not fired as are clay bricks, are even and fairly soft. They can be worked easily, but their colour, a greyish white, is not very interesting.

Clay bricks, which account for the vast majority, are fired in a kiln. They vary enormously both in quality and in colour and some are quite unsuitable for carving. A soft, evenly-textured brick is best, but it must be remembered that very soft bricks deteriorate after a number of years when exposed to the weather. If adequate information as to quality is not obtainable from merchants, tests should be carried out to check hardness and evenness of quality before buying.

With a little experience it is quite easy to spot suitable bricks, and, especially for children's work, odd bricks may be found on demolition sites or obtained from building sites at little or no expense.

Where a wall is to be made for carving, the mortar should be of similar hardness to the brick: one part cement, one part lime (slaked lime, ie. calcium hydroxide) and six parts sand being the usual mix.

WORKING

Single bricks or walls can be carved with sharp stonecarving tools, files and rifflers. Large sculptures can be worked with a bush hammer (see p. 77).

Care has to be taken, as bricks may be split or chipped if worked carelessly but they are not difficult. Power tools (see p. 67 and fig. 94) are very satisfactory for use with brick, and sand and shot-blasting has also been used.

Acrylic

This material has been used much less than might be expected. Perhaps the cost of the material inhibits sculptors from using it for big sculptures. Acrylic has great beauty. Under its tradenames of Perspex and Plexiglass it is well known, and used for a wide variety of purposes, both industrial and domestic. It is usually used in sheets up to 10 mm. in thickness, in which form it can be used for small reliefs and ornaments, but the sculptor will probably require it in greater thickness.

It can be obtained up to 100–125 mm. without too much difficulty from merchants, but above that thickness it has to be made up specially. Off-cuts several inches thick, and also rod and thick tube, can sometimes be obtained from manufacturers who use the material a lot. It is obtainable both clear (plain or coloured) and opaque, in a wide variety of colours.

Manipulation

Acrylic can be sawn, carved with woodcarving tools, abraded and polished. It chips readily and a thin sheet can easily be cracked, so some care has to be taken in working it.

Use a fine saw—a hacksaw or tenon saw. It may be bandsawn with an appropriate blade, and if used with a circular saw a fine tungsten-tipped blade is best, giving a very fine, clean cut. If much heat is generated when sawing, the scurf (plastic sawdust) will tend to melt and stick back onto the block, but it can be removed without much trouble.

Carving with woodcarving gouges is quite straightforward. Tools must be kept sharp (see section on woodcarving p. 39, for care and use of tools).

Acrylic can be drilled. It is best to have the drill 'cut back' (ground down to make the point shallower). This prevents chipping and cracking when the drill breaks through.

The material is perhaps best abraded, and in this its working is similar to ivory (p. 31). File, rasp, riffler, Surform, abrasive paper (garnet, sand, wet-or-dry) are used. Some carvers leave gouge-marks untouched, but it can be worked with finer and finer grades of abrasive paper and then polished. Polishing is best done with a buff and polishing compound. For this an electric drill on a stand is ideal, used with a calico buff. The stick of polishing compound is held against the buff, so that some of the material is picked up, and the perspex is then held against the buff. It is wise to wear goggles or eyeshield, as particles of calico and compound tend to fly off and can get in the eyes.

Designing

The main feature of acrylic is the way it transmits light. After a little experimenting, these characteristics can be taken advantage of to produce works of great beauty. Opaque acrylic is quite different and has, perhaps, less potential. Nevertheless, when polished it can be very attractive. Black acrylic, for instance, has something of the quality of jet, but looks softer.

Pierced sculptures can be produced, and the material will support thin elements, so long as they are not too fragile. Heat will distort or melt acrylic, so care must be taken when buffing thin or delicate carving, otherwise the heat generated will damage or destroy it. It scratches easily, and scratch marks are taken off by abrading and polishing.

Foamed plastic

Expanded polystyrene, styrene foam, foamed polyurethane, can be carved as sculptures in their own right, or used as masters for casting.

They are obtained in sheet or block form of varying grades. Expanded polystyrene consists of small globules or beads cemented together, while the foamed plastics have a sponge-like texture. The material is often used for packaging for delicate equipment. Useful blocks can be had from this source. Colour is mostly white, but some kinds are manufactured in a limited range of colours.

The material can be sawn with a hacksaw blade, rasped, Surformed and glasspapered. One of the most widely-used methods of working it, is to cut or shape it with heated tools. Heat melts foamed plastic very readily. The simplest method is to heat a metal object—soldering iron, knife, etc.—in a flame and melt away parts not required. The tool should not be too hot, as the material melts very easily and will vanish in a quite unexpected way if care is not taken.

A tool consisting of a steel wire which is heated by an electric current can be bought or made, and is more easily controlled. Fine grades of foamed plastic can be sandpapered to a smooth finish.

It is painted with emulsion paint or ordinary household paint. Its characteristic of extreme lightness makes it generally unsuitable for use out of doors, where even a light wind becomes a major consideration as it is liable to damage if knocked or buffeted, but for indoor sculptures, especially of a temporary nature, it is a very useful medium.

Soap

Soap is not used very widely, although it could be quite a useful medium for sketch models. It is carved by children, however, especially the very young, because it is readily obtainable and easily worked. Simple tools, such as wood modelling tools, metal spatulas, knife, nail-file, etc. are used.

Nowadays large blocks of soap are difficult to find, but a number of blocks can be joined together either by smoothing sides, thoroughly wetting, then rubbing together and holding firmly in place until set; or by using a suitable adhesive such as sodium silicate (water-glass).

A fine, softish soap is best for carving. It will tend to dry out and crack with time, but this can be prevented or delayed by applying a coat or two of clear lacquer or varnish.

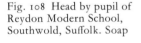
Fig. 108 Head by pupil of Reydon Modern School, Southwold, Suffolk. Soap

For further reading

Design
Animals in motion by Edweard Muybridge. Dover Publications Inc., New York
Form by Max Bill. Verlag Karl Werner, Basel
New design in wood by Donald Willcox. Van Nostrand, Reinhold Co., New York
The human figure in motion by Edweard Muybridge. Dover Publications Inc., New York
The man-made object. Edited by Gyorgy Kepes. Studio Vista, London and Braziller, New York
The origins of form in art by Herbert Read. Thames and Hudson, London 1965 and Horizon Press, New York

Drawing
Drawing lessons from the great masters by Hale. Studio Vista, London and Watson-Guptill, New York

Technical
Dictionary of building materials by William Kinniburgh. C. R. Books Ltd, 1966 (information about stone and wood, also all materials connected with building. A happy hunting ground for the inquisitive)
Ivory carving by Carson I. A. Ritchie. Arthur Barker Ltd, London 1969
The materials and methods of sculpture by Jack C. Rich. Oxford University Press (outlining most of the sculptor's materials and methods)
What wood is that? by Dr Alfred Schwankl, translated and edited by H. L. Edlin. Thames and Hudson, London 1956 and Viking Press, New York (an excellent text book on wood, containing actual timber samples)
Figure sculpture in wax and plaster by Richard McDermott Miller. Watson-Guptill Publications, New York
Plastics for artists and craftsmen by Harry B. Hollander. Watson-Guptill Publications, New York
Sculpture in plastics by Nicholas Roukes. Watson-Guptill Publications, New York
Wood design by Donald Willcox. Watson-Guptill Publications, New York

General
Constantin Brancusi by David Lewis. Alec Tiranti Ltd, London 1957
Jean Arp sculpture 1957–66 by Eduard Trier. Thames and Hudson, London and Abrams, New York
Gislebertus. Sculptor of Autun by Denis Grivet and George Zarnecki. Orion Press

This list could be extended indefinitely. There are many books on the works of the masters that can be obtained from libraries and good bookshops (e.g. A. Zwemmer Ltd, 78 Charing Cross Road, London WC2. Tiranti Bookshop, 72 Charlotte Street, London W1). In the US, some recommended art book stores are Wittenborn Art Books, 1018 Madison Ave., and E. Weye, Inc., 794 Lexington Ave., New York; Kroch's and Brentano's, 29 South Wabash, Chicago, Illinois; and Pickwick Bookshop, 6743 Hollywood Boulevard, Hollywood, California.

List of suppliers

Most tools and materials are readily available. The yellow-page telephone directory will give specialist firms, and a good tool merchant or hardware shop will supply many of the tools required.

Ivory
Material (*tusks, teeth, etc.*): F. Friedlein and Co. Ltd, Kudu House, The Minories, London EC3

Wood
Material: Thick pieces of hardwood may be difficult to find. Obtain from friends, farmers, local authority Parks Departments, etc., and season for yourself (a slow process). Or obtain from old furniture, or buy thick sections and glue together. Specialist timber merchants may be able to supply short lengths or offcuts, but many are not very willing to do so.
General Wood Supplies, 78 Stoke Newington High Street, London N16. The Hardwood Centre, W. C. Marshall Ltd, 2 Drysdale Street, London N1. and Shearman and Co. Ltd, Vicarage Road, Abbotskerswell, Newton Abbot, Devon (will sell short lengths).
Tools and equipment (*benches, chisels, gouges, etc.*): Parry and Sons (Tools) Ltd, 329 Old Street, London EC1.

S. Tyzak and Son Ltd, 341 Old Street, London EC1
Tools: Alec Tiranti Ltd, 72 Charlotte Street, London W1; Shearman and Co. Ltd (address above)

Stone
Material: The following merchants sell a wide range of stone: J. Bysouth, Dorset Road, Tottenham, London N15. William Allen (Croydon) Ltd, 150 Canterbury Road, Croydon, Surrey. Haines and Warwick Ltd, Old Church Road, Romford, Essex; Natural Stone Quarries Ltd, Springwell Quarries, Gateshead, Co. Durham.
The British Stone Federation, Alderman House, 37 Soho Square, London W1 will send you a list of their members with addresses and what stones they sell
Tools (making and remaking): J. Grimes, 27 Chippenham Mews, London W9. Eastway Tool Service, 39 Chamber Street, London E1. Or ask your nearest mason's yard or quarry where they have their tools remade and resharpened
Tool suppliers: good toolsmiths, for instance: Buck and Ryan, 101 Tottenham Court Road, London W1 (try to go in person, as this is more satisfactory). Alec Tiranti Ltd (address above, supplies most carving tools and equipment for both wood and stone, as well as having an excellent bookshop specializing in arts, crafts and architecture). Shearman and Co. Ltd (address above, supplies wood and stone-carving tools and equipment and also small pieces of stone including rough lumps of alabaster, soapstone, etc., and pieces of wood suitable for carving.) Alec Tiranti Ltd, and Shearman and Co. Ltd will send a catalogue and price list on request.

Plaster
Material: Artists suppliers sell fine plaster in small quantities, but this is an expensive way of buying plaster. If much work is to be done, it is worth ordering a bag (112 lbs) from a merchant. Be sure to store dry, for instance in a polyethylene bag.
Terrey Bros. Ltd, Plaster Merchants, 58 Andalus Road, London SW9. East London Builders' Merchant Supplies, Plaster Distributors, 274 Poyser Street, London E2
Tools: good tool shops and Alec Tiranti Ltd (address above)

Aeriated concrete building blocks
Brand names in UK are Cencon, Durox, Siporex and Thermalite. Obtain from builders' merchants and information from manufacturers (e.g. Thermalite, Hams Hall, Lea Marston, Sutton Coldfield, Warwickshire)

Brick
Obtain from builders' merchants and information from Redland Bricks Ltd, Graylands, Horsham, Sussex

Acrylic
G. H. Bloore Ltd, Honeypot Lane, Stanmore, Middlesex. ICI, Welwyn Garden City, Hertfordshire. Try manufacturers of acrylic goods for offcuts

Expanded polystyrene
Do-it-yourself shops, decorators, etc. in fairly thin sheets. R. Passmore and Co. Ltd, 12 Narrow Street, London E14 (up to 125–150 mm. (5–6 ins) thick)

US art materials suppliers

Carving materials, wood, stone, plaster
Sculpture Associates, Ltd, 114 East 25 Street, New York, NY 10010.
Sculpture House, 38 East 30 Street, New York, NY 10016.
Sculpture Services, Inc., 9 East 19 Street, New York, NY 10003

Art supplies, tools, plaster
A. I. Friedman, Inc., 25 West 45 Street, New York, NY 10036
Art Brown & Bro., Inc., 2 West 46 Street, New York, NY 10036

Acrylic and expanded polystyrene
Resin Coatings Corporation, 14940 NW 25 Court, Opa Locka, Florida 33054.
Polyproducts Corporation, Order Department, Room 25, 13810 Nelson Ave., Detroit, Michigan 48227

Building blocks and bricks
Local building materials suppliers.

Index